MATH Trailblazers

A BALANCED MATHEMATICS PROGRAM INTEGRATING SCIENCE AND LANGUAGE ARTS

Unit Resource Guide
Unit 7

Exploring Multiplicaton and Division

THIRD EDITION

KENDALL/HUNT PUBLISHING COMPANY
4050 Westmark Drive   Dubuque, Iowa 52002

A TIMS® Curriculum
University of Illinois at Chicago

UIC The University of Illinois
at Chicago

The original edition was based on work supported by the National Science Foundation under grant No. MDR 9050226 and the University of Illinois at Chicago. Any opinions, findings, and conclusions or recommendations expressed in this publication are those of the author(s) and do not necessarily reflect the views of the granting agencies.

Letter Home

Exploring Multiplication and Division

Date: _____

Dear Family Member:

During this unit your child will encounter multiplication and division problems in real-world situations and connect to other areas of mathematics. For example, after reading a recipe, your child will use multiplication and a graph to figure out how many lemons are needed to make six pitchers of lemonade. Students will use division to determine how many cupcakes each person at a birthday party will get. These and other real-world problems help them see multiplication and division as part of their everyday lives.

You can provide additional support at home.

- **Make Lemonade.** You and your child can make lemonade, following this recipe or one of your own. Ask your child what you would need to do to double or triple the recipe.

- **Subtraction Facts.** Help your child prepare for a quiz on the subtraction facts in Groups 1 and 2 using the flash cards.

Thank you for continuing to work with your child on mathematics concepts at home.

Sincerely,

_____

Homemade Lemonade

Ingredients
Juice from 8 lemons
2 quarts of cold water
1 cup sugar

Instructions
1. Combine all ingredients in a large (2-quart) pitcher.
2. Stir well to dissolve the sugar completely.
3. Pour over ice cubes.

Makes one 2-quart pitcher.

Mathematics in the real world

Carta al hogar

Investigando la multiplicación y la división

Fecha: _____

Estimado miembro de familia:

Durante esta unidad su hijo/a se encontrará con problemas de multiplicación y división de situaciones de la vida real y que se relacionan con otras áreas de las matemáticas. Por ejemplo, después de leer una receta, su hijo/a usará la multiplicación y una gráfica para averiguar cuántos limones se necesitan para hacer seis jarras de limonada. Los estudiantes usarán la división para determinar cuántos pastelitos recibirá cada persona en una fiesta de cumpleaños. Estos y otros problemas de la vida real ayudarán a su hijo/a a entender que la multiplicación y la división son parte de nuestras vidas cotidianas.

Usted puede proporcionar apoyo adicional en casa.

- **Hacer limonada.** Usted y su hijo/a puede hacer limonada, usando esta receta o una receta propia. Pregúntele a su hijo/a qué se necesita hacer para duplicar o triplicar la receta.

- **Restas básicas.** Ayude a su hijo/a a prepararse para un examen sobre las restas básicas de los grupos 1 y 2 usando las tarjetas.

Limonada casera

Ingredientes
Jugo de 8 limones
2 cuartos de galón de agua fría
1 taza de azúcar

Instrucciones
1. Combine todos los ingredientes en una jarra grande (de 2 cuartos de galón).
2. Revuelva bien para disolver el azúcar completamente.
3. Sirva sobre hielo.

Esta receta rinde una jarra de dos cuartos de galón.

Matemáticas en la vida real

Gracias por seguir practicando los conceptos matemáticos con su hijo/a en casa.

Atentamente,

_____

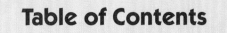

Table of Contents

Unit 7
Exploring Multiplication and Division

Unit 7

Outline
Exploring Multiplication and Division

Unit Summary

Estimated Class Sessions
11-12

Students continue to develop their conceptual understanding of multiplication and division and use graphs to explore multiples. To do this, students collect and graph data. This is students' first experience making point graphs. Students work with a recipe for lemonade and use multiplication, division, and graphing to solve problems related to increasing quantities in the recipe.

Mathhoppers, imaginary creatures that jump specified numbers of units on a number line, help students explore multiplication and division concepts.

Students use the division symbol when they solve problems in the context of planning a birthday party. In the culminating activity, students investigate the multiplicative relationship between the number of sides of a regular figure and its perimeter. They measure a side and the perimeter of the figures, record and graph the data, and analyze the results using multiplication and division.

The DPP for this unit reviews and assesses the subtraction facts in Groups 1 and 2 and develops strategies for learning the last six multiplication facts (4×6, 4×7, 4×8, 6×7, 6×8, 7×8).

Major Concept Focus

- multiplication concepts
- division concepts
- multiplication as repeated addition
- division as repeated subtraction
- multiplication sentences
- division sentences
- interpreting remainders
- graphing and analyzing data
- point graphs
- number lines
- measuring length in centimeters
- perimeter of polygons
- investigating patterns
- communicating problem-solving solutions
- assessing problem solving
- Student Rubric: *Telling*
- subtraction facts review and assessment for Groups 1 and 2
- strategies for the last six multiplication facts

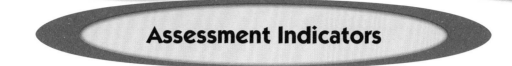

Assessment Indicators

Use the following Assessment Indicators and the *Observational Assessment Record* that follows the Background section in this unit to assess students on key ideas.

A1. Can students represent multiplication and division using manipulatives, number lines, data tables, graphs, pictures, and words?

A2. Can students write number sentences for multiplication and division situations?

A3. Can students solve multiplication and division problems and explain their reasoning?

A4. Can students make and interpret point graphs?

A5. Can students use patterns in data tables and graphs to make predictions and solve problems?

A6. Can students find the perimeter of regular shapes?

A7. Can students solve problems involving money?

A8. Do students demonstrate fluency with the subtraction facts in Groups 1 and 2?

Unit Planner

KEY: SG = Student Guide, DAB = Discovery Assignment Book, AB = Adventure Book, URG = Unit Resource Guide, DPP = Daily Practice and Problems, HP = Home Practice (found in Discovery Assignment Book), and TIG = Teacher Implementation Guide.

	Lesson Information	Supplies	Copies/Transparencies
Lesson 1 **Lemonade Stand** URG Pages 26–45 SG Pages 82–85 DAB Pages 115–118 DPP A–D *Estimated Class Sessions* **2**	**Activity** Students use multiplication, division, and graphing to solve problems involving a recipe for lemonade. The activity introduces point graphs. **Math Facts** DPP items A, B, and C provide practice with math facts. **Homework** 1. Assign the *Mr. Green's Giant Gumball Jamboree* Homework Pages in the *Discovery Assignment Book.* 2. Students study the subtraction facts in Group 1 at home using their flash cards. **Assessment** Use *Mr. Green's Giant Gumball Jamboree* and the *Observational Assessment Record* to note students' abilities to make and interpret point graphs.	• 1 ruler per student • lemons, sugar, water, paper cups, and a pitcher to make and serve lemonade, optional	• 1 copy of *Two-column Data Table* URG Page 37 per student • 2 copies of *Centimeter Graph Paper* URG Page 38 per student • 1 copy of *Subtraction Flash Cards: Group 1* URG Pages 39–40, copied back to back per student, optional • 1 transparency of *Lemonade Stand Graph* URG Page 41 • 1 transparency of *What Went Wrong?* URG Page 42 • 1 copy of *Observational Assessment Record* URG Pages 13–14 to be used throughout this unit
Lesson 2 **Katie's Job** URG Pages 46–56 DPP E–F HP Parts 1–2 *Estimated Class Sessions* **1-2**	**Assessment Activity** Students work individually or in groups to solve problems using a graph and multiplication and division. They are introduced to the *Telling* rubric as a guide for their work. **Math Facts** Task F provides computation and facts practice. **Homework** Assign Parts 1 and 2 of the Home Practice. **Assessment** 1. Score student work using the Telling dimension of the *TIMS Multidimensional Rubric.* 2. Add the completed work to student portfolios.	• 1 calculator per student • 1 ruler per student	• 1 copy of *Katie's Job* URG Pages 53–54 per student • 1 transparency of *Katie's Job* URG Pages 53–54, optional • 1 copy of *TIMS Multidimensional Rubric* TIG, Assessment section • 1 transparency or poster of TIMS Student Rubric: *Telling* TIG, Assessment section, optional
Lesson 3 **Mathhoppers** URG Pages 57–69 SG Pages 86–89 DAB Pages 119–121 DPP G–J HP Part 3 *Estimated Class Sessions* **2**	**Activity** Mathhoppers are creatures that can jump a specified number of units on a number line. Students solve mathhopper problems that further their study of multiplication and division. They connect multiplication to repeated addition and division to repeated subtraction. **Math Facts** DPP items G and I provide practice with math facts. **Homework** 1. Assign the *Professor Peabody's Mathhoppers* Homework Page. 2. Assign Part 3 of the Home Practice. 3. Students study the subtraction facts in Group 2 at home using their flash cards.	• 1 meterstick or measuring tape (for use as a number line) per student group • 1 green pattern block or other marker (for use as a mathhopper) per student group • about 60 centimeter connecting cubes per student group and some for the teacher • 1 pair of scissors per student	• 1 copy of *Subtraction Flash Cards: Group 2* URG Pages 65–66, per student copied back to back, optional • 1 transparency of the first *Mathhoppers* Activity Page SG Page 86

	Lesson Information	Supplies	Copies/ Transparencies
	Assessment Use the *Observational Assessment Record* to record students' abilities to represent multiplication and division using manipulatives, number lines, and words and to write number sentences for multiplication.	• 1 calculator per student • tape	
Lesson 4 **Birthday Party** URG Pages 70–77 SG Pages 90–92 DPP K–N *Estimated Class Sessions* **2**	**Activity** Using the context of a birthday party, students work on a variety of problems they can solve using division. The division symbol is introduced. **Homework** Assign the Homework section of the *Birthday Party* Activity Pages. **Assessment** Use journal entries to assess students' abilities to communicate their solution strategies and represent multiplication and division using manipulatives, number lines, and other tools.	• 30 or more counters per student pair • 1 calculator per student	
Lesson 5 **The Money Jar** URG Pages 78–88 SG Pages 93–94 DPP O–P *Estimated Class Sessions* **1**	**Activity** Students solve a series of problems in which they must decide how to divide money equally among the members of a family. They write division number sentences to show their solutions. **Math Facts** DPP Task P provides practice with division. **Homework** Assign the homework problems on *The Money Jar* Activity Pages. **Assessment** 1. Use DPP Task P to assess students' understanding of division. 2. Use the *Observational Assessment Record* to note students' abilities to represent division using manipulatives.	• play money: 60 pennies, 50 dimes, and 10 nickels per student • 1 calculator per student • scissors, optional	• 1 copy of *Money Masters* URG Pages 85–87 per student group to substitute for play money, optional
Lesson 6 **Walking around Shapes** URG Pages 89–102 DAB Pages 123–128 DPP Q–V HP Part 4 *Estimated Class Sessions* **3**	**Activity** Students investigate the relationship between the length of a side and the perimeter of regular polygons, using data tables and line graphs. They use the patterns they find to solve problems, working with multiples of 3, 4, 5, and 6. **Math Facts** DPP Bit Q practices math facts. Bit U is a quiz on subtraction facts. **Homework** 1. Assign the *Walking around Squares* Homework Pages. 2. Assign Part 4 of the Home Practice.	• 1 ruler per student	• 1 copy of *Subtraction Facts Quiz A* URG Page 25 per student • 1 copy of *Professor Peabody's Shapes Data* URG Page 98 per student • 3 copies of *Centimeter Graph Paper* URG Page 38 per student • 1 transparency of *Walking around Triangles* DAB Page 124 • 1 transparency of *Centimeter Graph Paper* URG Page 38

(Continued)

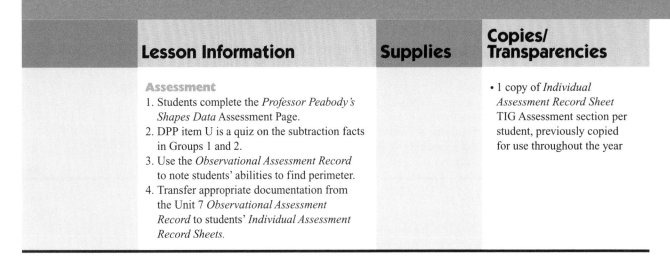

Lesson Information	Supplies	Copies/Transparencies
Assessment 1. Students complete the *Professor Peabody's Shapes Data* Assessment Page. 2. DPP item U is a quiz on the subtraction facts in Groups 1 and 2. 3. Use the *Observational Assessment Record* to note students' abilities to find perimeter. 4. Transfer appropriate documentation from the Unit 7 *Observational Assessment Record* to students' *Individual Assessment Record Sheets.*		• 1 copy of *Individual Assessment Record Sheet* TIG Assessment section per student, previously copied for use throughout the year

Connections

A current list of literature and software connections is available at *www.mathtrailblazers.com.* You can also find information on connections in the *Teacher Implementation Guide* Literature List and Software List sections.

Literature Connections
Suggested Titles

- Billin-Frye, Paige. *Everybody Wins!* The Kane Press, New York, 2001.
- Burns, Marilyn. *Spaghetti and Meatballs for All!* Scholastic Press, New York, 1997.
- Murphy, Stuart J. *Divide and Ride.* Harper Collins Publishers, New York, 1997.
- Pinczes, Elinor. *A Remainder of One.* Houghton Mifflin Company, Boston, MA, 1995.
- Schwartz, David. *If You Hopped Like a Frog.* Scholastic Press, New York, 1999.
- Silverstein, Shel. "Smart." In *Where the Sidewalk Ends,* p. 35. Harper Collins Children's Books, New York, 1974. (Lesson 5)
- Stamper, Judith Bauer. *Breakfast At Danny's Diner.* Grosset and Dunlap, New York, 2003.

Software Connections

- *Graphers* is a data graphing tool appropriate for young students.
- *Ice Cream Truck* develops problem solving, money skills, and arithmetic operations.
- *Mighty Math Calculating Crew* poses short answer questions about number operations and money.
- *Money Challenge* provides practice with money.
- *National Library of Virtual Manipulatives* website (http://matti.usu.edu) allows students to work with manipulatives including rectangular arrays, number lines, and bar graphs.
- *Penny Pot* provides practice with counting coins.

Teaching All Math Trailblazers Students

Math Trailblazers® lessons are designed for students with a wide range of abilities. The lessons are flexible and do not require significant adaptation for diverse learning styles or academic levels. However, when needed, lessons can be tailored to allow students to engage their abilities to the greatest extent possible while building knowledge and skills.

To assist you in meeting the needs of all students in your classroom, this section contains information about some of the features in the curriculum that allow all students access to mathematics. For additional information, see the Teaching the *Math Trailblazers* Student: Meeting Individual Needs section in the *Teacher Implementation Guide.*

Differentiation Opportunities in this Unit

Journal Prompts

Journal prompts provide opportunities for students to explain and reflect on mathematical problems. They can help both students who need practice explaining their ideas and students who benefit from answering higher order questions. Students with various learning styles can express themselves using pictures, words, and sentences. Teachers can alter journal prompts to suit students' ability levels. The following lessons contain a journal prompt:

- Lesson 1 *Lemonade Stand*
- Lesson 3 *Mathhoppers*
- Lesson 4 *Birthday Party*
- Lesson 5 *The Money Jar*
- Lesson 6 *Walking around Shapes*

Extensions

Use extensions to enrich lessons. Many extensions provide opportunities to further involve or challenge students of all abilities. Take a moment to review the extensions prior to beginning this unit. Some extensions may require additional preparation and planning. The following lessons contain extensions:

- Lesson 1 *Lemonade Stand*
- Lesson 3 *Mathhoppers*
- Lesson 6 *Walking around Shapes*

Background
Exploring Multiplication and Division

This unit's activities continue the study of multiplication and division. Students encounter many types of multiplication and division problems, discover different strategies for solving problems, and learn to communicate their solutions in many ways. For example, students use graphs to explore multiplication and division in Lesson 1 *Lemonade Stand* and number lines in Lesson 3 *Mathhoppers*. Lesson 4 *Birthday Party* and Lesson 5 *The Money Jar* introduce other division situations and explore interpreting remainders. Finally, Lesson 6 *Walking around Shapes* integrates multiplication, division, and graphing into an investigation of the relationship between the perimeter and length of one side of regular polygons.

The problems in this unit use simple fractions as well as whole numbers. By introducing multiplication and division with fractions at this early stage, we hope to avoid misconceptions that students often develop when they multiply and divide solely with whole numbers. For example, one problem asks students to share six pizzas equally among twelve people. Using pictures and their knowledge of the world, they can find that each person will receive $\frac{1}{2}$ pizza. The resulting number sentence, $6 \div 12 = \frac{1}{2}$, emphasizes the fact that a smaller number can be divided by a larger number. Also, it acquaints students with the notion that fractions denote division: $6 \div 12$ can be represented as $\frac{6}{12}$, which is equivalent to $\frac{1}{2}$.

Types of Multiplication and Division Problems

Researchers who have studied multiplication and division have identified different types of multiplication and division problems. While students do not need to be able to identify these different types of problems by name, it is important that they encounter and solve them. The sections that follow show the different types of multiplication and

division problems, all of which are included in our third-grade curriculum.

Problems Involving a Number of Equal Groups

The problems involved in *Making Teams* (Unit 3 Lesson 4) are good examples. Using the same situation, three different questions emerge. One question is interpreted as a multiplication problem, the other two as division problems.

- The unknown is the total number in all the groups: If there are 5 teams with 4 members on each team, how many players are there in all? There are two known factors and a missing product. Using established knowledge, students often interpret this correctly as a repeated addition problem ($4 + 4 + 4 + 4 + 4 = 20$). Through classroom experiences with many such problems, they connect the repeated addition sentence to a **multiplication** sentence ($5 \times 4 = 20$).

- The unknown is the number of groups: Twenty members of a class are divided into teams of 4 members each. How many teams are there? The problem gives the total number in all the groups and the measure or size of each group. This aspect of division is called **measurement division.**

- The unknown is the number in each group: Twenty class members are divided equally into 5 teams. How many students are on each team? The problem gives the total number of students and the number of groups or partitions. This aspect of division is known as **partitive division.**

Jumps on a number line and arrays provide additional experiences with multiplication and division with equal groups. Successive jumps of equal size on a number line, introduced in this unit using mythical creatures called mathhoppers, provide a model for multiplication as repeated addition and division as repeated subtraction. An **array,** which is introduced in a later unit, is a group of objects arranged in rows and columns.

Problems Involving Scale Factors

This type of problem is often found in TIMS laboratory experiments. For example, after students roll three different cars down a ramp, you might ask whether one car rolled three times as far as another. Similarly, when finding the mass of objects, you may ask whether the mass of one object is one-half the mass of another object.

A Cartesian Product

This type of problem asks for the number of possible pairs that can be made from two sets. For example, if one is a set of two shirts and the other is a set of three pants, the problem is to find all six possible shirt-pant pairs. Young children are able to solve this type of problem using manipulatives and diagrams.

It is not important for students to identify the problem types by name. However, experiences with many types of problems will provide a strong conceptual foundation not only for multiplication and division, but also for fractions, ratios, and proportional reasoning.

Notes on Graphing

The graphing techniques in this unit are an integral part of *Math Trailblazers*. They are powerful tools for studying many of the big ideas students will encounter in their study of mathematics, especially algebraic concepts. In this unit students learn to represent data using point graphs as well as bar graphs. In the activities *Lemonade Stand* and *Walking around Shapes,* they use point graphs to investigate multiplication and division. As the curriculum progresses, students will use the same techniques to analyze more sophisticated concepts, such as proportional reasoning and functions.

In subsequent units students will choose which kind of graph is the most appropriate to use in a given situation. Since a graph is a visual representation of the relationship between variables, the appropriateness of the graph depends on the type of variables in the experiment. Up to this point, students have used bar graphs to represent data and study the relationships between variables. Often, the pairs of variables we study have included a quantitative variable and a qualitative variable, e.g., area and type of towels. Figure 1 shows the graph from *The Better "Picker Upper"* in Unit 5. The horizontal axis is labeled with the various types of paper towels. The values for the type of towels are discrete; that is, there are no

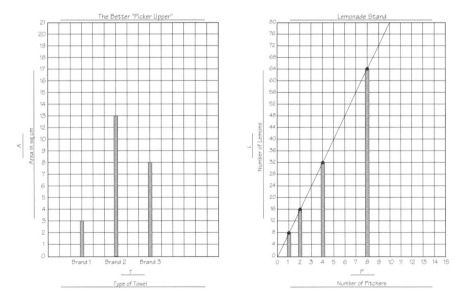

Figure 1: *A bar graph for qualitative variables and a point graph for quantitative, nondiscrete variables*

values between the types of towels. Thus, it does not make much sense to connect them with a line. A bar graph is the appropriate type of graph for representing this type of data.

When both variables to be graphed are quantitative, a point graph is sometimes the appropriate way to represent the data. This type of data is found in the activity *Lemonade Stand,* where the context of making and selling lemonade allows us to study the relationship between two quantitative variables: number of pitchers and number of lemons. Since the values for both of these variables are numbers and since the values for the number of pitchers, unlike those for types of towels, are not discrete—that is, there are values between the data points, such as 3, $3\frac{1}{2}$, 7, or $7\frac{1}{2}$ pitchers—it is possible to use points instead of bars to represent the data. Drawing a line or a curve through the points makes sense only when the data points form a pattern and when there are legitimate values between the data points.

Lemonade Stand is students' first exposure to point graphs. To simplify students' initial attempts at graphing, they graph the data on a bar graph first and then convert the bar graph to a point graph. Students find that the points fall on a straight line and use a ruler to draw the line passing through them, as shown in Figure 1. Later, this line becomes the basis for making predictions about values that lie between and beyond the data points.

Although point graphs are often used when both variables are quantitative, that is not always the case. The two variables in the experiment *First Names* in Unit 1 are number of letters and number of students. While both of these variables are quantitative, they are also discrete—that is, it is not meaningful to speak of $6\frac{1}{2}$ letters in a name or $6\frac{1}{2}$ people who have that number of letters in their names. Thus, we can see why a line on a point graph, in which values between data points are represented, would not be appropriate for quantitative, discrete variables. The data in *First Names,* therefore, is best represented on a bar graph. See Figure 2.

For more information, see the TIMS Tutor: *The TIMS Laboratory Method* in the *Teacher Implementation Guide.*

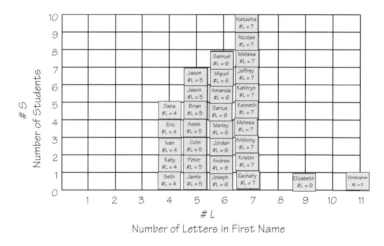

Figure 2: *A bar graph for quantitative, discrete variables*

Resources

- Anghileri, Julie, and David C. Johnson. "Arithmetic Operations on Whole Numbers: Multiplication and Division." In *Teaching Mathematics in Grades K through 8: Research-Based Methods*, Thomas R. Post, ed., pp. 146–189. Allyn and Bacon, Needham Heights, MA, 1992.

- Burns, Marilyn. "Introducing Division through Problem-Solving Experiences." In *The Arithmetic Teacher: Mathematics Education through the Middle Grades* (April 1991, pp. 14–18). National Council of Teachers of Mathematics, Reston, VA, 1991.

- Carpenter, T.P., E. Fennema, M.L. Franke, L. Levi, and S.E. Empson. *Children's Mathematics: Cognitively Guided Instruction.* Heinemann, Westport, CT, 1999.

- Page, David A. *Maneuvers on Number Lines.* Education Development Center, Newton, MA, 1976.

- Rothmell, Edward C., and Paul R. Trafton. "Whole Number Computation." In *Mathematics for the Young Child.* National Council of Teachers of Mathematics, Reston, VA, 1990.

Observational Assessment Record

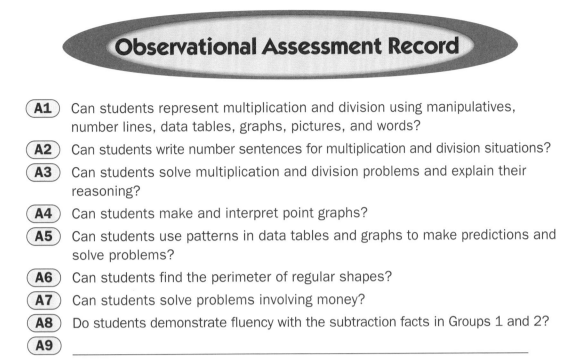

A1 Can students represent multiplication and division using manipulatives, number lines, data tables, graphs, pictures, and words?

A2 Can students write number sentences for multiplication and division situations?

A3 Can students solve multiplication and division problems and explain their reasoning?

A4 Can students make and interpret point graphs?

A5 Can students use patterns in data tables and graphs to make predictions and solve problems?

A6 Can students find the perimeter of regular shapes?

A7 Can students solve problems involving money?

A8 Do students demonstrate fluency with the subtraction facts in Groups 1 and 2?

A9 _____

Name	A1	A2	A3	A4	A5	A6	A7	A8	A9	Comments
1.										
2.										
3.										
4.										
5.										
6.										
7.										
8.										
9.										
10.										
11.										
12.										

Name	A1	A2	A3	A4	A5	A6	A7	A8	A9	Comments
13										
14.										
15.										
16.										
17.										
18.										
19.										
20.										
21.										
22.										
23.										
24.										
25.										
26.										
27.										
28.										
29.										
30.										
31.										
32.										

Unit 7

Daily Practice and Problems
Exploring Multiplication and Division

A DPP Menu for Unit 7

Two Daily Practice and Problems (DPP) items are included for each class session listed in the Unit Outline. A scope and sequence chart for the DPP is in the *Teacher Implementation Guide*.

Icons in the Teacher Notes column designate the subject matter of each DPP item. The first item in each class session is always a Bit and the second is either a Task or Challenge. Each item falls into one or more of the categories listed below. A menu of the DPP items for Unit 7 follows.

N **Number Sense** E, H, J, R, S	※ **Computation** D, F, M, S, T, V	🕐 **Time** E, K, L	**Geometry** N, O
⁵⁄₇ **Math Facts** A–C, F, G, I, P, Q, U	$ **Money** F	**Measurement**	**Data**

Practicing and Assessing the Subtraction Facts

In this unit students review and are assessed on the subtraction facts in Groups 1 and 2. Effective strategies for these groups are using a ten, making a ten, and reasoning from known addition facts. DPP Bits C and I remind students to practice with their *Subtraction Flash Cards: Group 1* and *Subtraction Flash Cards: Group 2*. DPP Bits A and G provide practice. *Subtraction Facts Quiz A* is assigned in Bit U. Students should update their *Subtraction Facts I Know* charts after taking the quiz.

Subtraction Flash Cards: Group 1 and *2* were distributed in the *Discovery Assignment Book* in Unit 2. Blackline masters for Groups 1 and 2 flashcards are available in Lessons 1 and 3, respectively, and for all groups in the *Grade 3 Facts Resource Guide.*

Developing Strategies for the Multiplication Facts

DPP items in this unit develop strategies for the multiplication facts for the last six facts: 4×6, 4×7, 4×8, 6×7, 6×8, 7×8. See DPP items B, F, P, and Q for work with these facts. Item P provides practice with multiplication using related division facts.

For information on the practice and assessment of subtraction facts in Grade 3, see the Lesson Guide for Unit 2 Lesson 7 *Assessing the Subtraction Facts.* For information on the study of the multiplication facts in Grade 3, see the Daily Practice and Problems Guide for Units 3 and 11. For a detailed explanation of our approach to learning and assessing the math facts in Grade 3, see the *Grade 3 Facts Resource Guide,* and for information for Grades K–5, see the TIMS Tutor: *Math Facts* in the *Teacher Implementation Guide.*

Students may solve the items individually, in groups, or as a class. The items may also be assigned for homework. The DPPs are also available on the Teacher Resource CD.

Student Questions	Teacher Notes

A Subtraction Facts: Group 1

Do the following problems in your head. Write only the answers.

1. $12 - 10 =$

2. $13 - 10 =$

3. $15 - 10 =$

4. $12 - 9 =$

5. $13 - 9 =$

6. $15 - 9 =$

7. $19 - 10 =$

8. $13 - 4 =$

9. $15 - 6 =$

TIMS Bit

1. 2	2. 3
3. 5	4. 3
5. 4	6. 6
7. 9	8. 9
9. 9	

Students begin a review of each of the Subtraction Facts Groups. (See the Unit 2 Lesson 7 Lesson Guide for an outline of the study of the facts throughout the year.) To focus practice on this group, students should work with the flash cards for Group 1 only. These facts focus on using a ten and thinking addition. Discuss these and other strategies that help students with these facts and ask them to practice using the strategies at home.

B Story Solving

1. Write a story and draw a picture about 8×7. Write a number sentence on your picture.

2. Write a story and draw a picture about 8×4. Write a number sentence on your picture.

TIMS Task

Students can share their stories with the class. If a computer with a drawing program is available, students may choose to draw their pictures on the computer.

Student Questions	Teacher Notes

C **Subtraction Flash Cards: Group 1**

1. With a partner, sort the *Subtraction Flash Cards: Group 1* into three stacks: Facts I Know Quickly, Facts I Know Using a Strategy, and Facts I Need to Learn.

2. Update your *Subtraction Facts I Know* chart. Circle the facts you answered quickly. Underline those you know by using a strategy. Do nothing to those you still need to learn.

TIMS Bit $\boxed{\begin{smallmatrix} 5 \\ \times 7 \end{smallmatrix}}$

Have students sort *Subtraction Flash Cards: Group 1*. After students sort, they should update the *Subtraction Facts I Know* chart. Students can take the cards for Group 1 home to practice with their families. The flash cards for Group 1 were distributed in the *Discovery Assignment Book* in Unit 2. These flash cards are available in Lesson 1 and in the *Grade 3 Facts Resource Guide*.

D **Messy Student**

A messy student spilled some ink on a math paper. These problems got ink on them. Can you figure out the numbers that got covered up?

1. $\begin{array}{r} \overset{1}{4}7 \\ + 38 \\ \hline \end{array}$ 2. $\begin{array}{r} \overset{1}{2} \\ + 65 \\ \hline 93 \end{array}$ 3. $\begin{array}{r} \\ + 24 \\ \hline 90 \end{array}$

TIMS Task

1. 85
2. 8
3. 66

E **Calculator Counting by 20s**

Work with a partner. One partner counts. The other times the counting partner. Then, switch jobs and count again.

Predict how long it will take to count by 20s to 1000. Use a calculator to count by 20s to 1000. Say the numbers quietly to yourself. How long did it take?

TIMS Bit

Pressing 20 + 20 = = on a calculator with an addition constant will cause many calculators to count by 20s. Before using this bit, try the problem on your calculator so you know the precise keystrokes that work for your model.

Discuss the patterns students notice as they count or discuss the predictions they made.

F Candy Bars

1. Mr. Green sells candy bars for 60¢ each. How much will 8 candy bars cost?

2. Marge spent $4.20 on candy bars at Mr. Green's store. How many candy bars did she buy?

TIMS Task $ x⁵⁷ ✕⃫

1. $4.80

2. 7 candy bars

G Subtraction Facts: Group 2

Do the following problems in your head. Write only the answers.

1. $14 - 10 =$

2. $16 - 10 =$

3. $17 - 10 =$

4. $14 - 9 =$

5. $16 - 9 =$

6. $17 - 9 =$

7. $14 - 5 =$

8. $16 - 7 =$

9. $11 - 9 =$

TIMS Bit x⁵⁷

1. 4
2. 6
3. 7
4. 5
5. 7
6. 8
7. 9
8. 9
9. 2

Ask students to use *Subtraction Flash Cards: Group 2* to study these facts, applying appropriate strategies for learning the facts. Possible strategies include using a ten and thinking addition.

H **Base-Ten Pieces**

1. Show the number 3602 with base-ten pieces. Use the Fewest Pieces Rule.

2. Show this number with base-ten shorthand.

TIMS Task Ⓝ

This is a review of the place value concepts students worked on in Unit 6.

1. 3 packs, 6 flats, 2 bits

2.

I **Subtraction Flash Cards: Group 2**

1. With a partner, sort the *Subtraction Flash Cards: Group 2* into three stacks: Facts I Know Quickly, Facts I Know Using a Strategy, and Facts I Need to Learn.

2. Update your *Subtraction Facts I Know* chart. Circle the facts you answered quickly. Underline those you know by using a strategy. Do nothing to those you still need to learn.

TIMS Bit $\frac{5}{\times 7}$

Have students sort *Subtraction Flash Cards: Group 2* and update their *Subtraction Facts I Know* charts. Have students take the cards for Group 2 home to practice with their families. The flash cards for Group 2 were distributed in the *Discovery Assignment Book* in Unit 2. The cards are also available in Lesson 3 and the *Grade 3 Facts Resource Guide*.

Tell students when you will give *Subtraction Facts Quiz A*, which is made up of facts from Groups 1 and 2. After the quiz, students should update their *Subtraction Facts I Know* charts. Quiz A is in this unit's TIMS Bit U.

Student Questions	Teacher Notes

J The Number 908 Is . . . .

The number 908 is . . .

A. 10 more than _____

B. 10 less than _____

C. 100 more than _____

D. 100 less than _____

E. about half of _____

F. about twice _____

G. 800 + _____

H. about 10 × _____

I. 500 + _____

J. 110 less than _____

TIMS Task   N

After students write down their answers, let them discuss their strategies, as well as their answers, in groups or as a class.

A. 898

B. 918

C. 808

D. 1008

E. 1800

F. 450

(Answers may vary for E, F, and H.)

G. 108

H. 90

I. 408

J. 1018

K Counting by Half Hours

Count by half hours beginning with 7:00 A.M. and ending at 7:00 P.M. Begin like this:

7:00, 7:30, 8:00, 8:30, 9:00 . . .

TIMS Bit

Students can use counting by half hours to help them solve problems involving elapsed time. (See TIMS Task L.)

L Time

How long have you been awake today?

How long have you been in school?

How long is it until the bell rings the next time?

TIMS Task

Students can count hours and half hours to help solve the problems. Encourage students to give their answers to the nearest half hour whenever appropriate.

Student Questions	Teacher Notes

(M) **Shortcut Addition and Subtraction**

Do the following problems using a shortcut method. You may use base-ten shorthand if you wish.

1. 241
   + 83

2. 517
   − 45

3. 5479
   + 4067

4. 4005
   − 3975

5. Explain a way to do Question 4 using mental math.

TIMS Bit

1. 324

2. 472

3. 9546

4. 30

5. Possible strategy: Count up by fives from 3975 to 4005 for a difference of 30.

(N) **Triangles, Hexagons, and Pentagons**

Here is a regular triangle, a regular hexagon, and a regular pentagon. In a regular shape, all the sides are the same length and all the angles are equal.

Draw a triangle that is not a regular triangle.

Draw a hexagon that is not a regular hexagon.

Draw a pentagon that is not a regular pentagon.

TIMS Task

Students will work with regular figures in the activity *Walking around Shapes* in Lesson 6.

Student Questions	Teacher Notes

⦿ Regular Rectangles

Draw a regular rectangle. Remember all the sides are equal in a regular shape.

What is another name for a regular rectangle?

TIMS Bit

Squares are regular rectangles.

Ⓟ Sharing Muffins

1. You want to share 24 muffins equally among 6 friends. How many muffins does each person get?

2. Two friends move away. You want to share 24 muffins equally among 4 friends. How many muffins does each person get?

3. The dog ate 3 muffins. You want to share 21 muffins equally among 6 friends. How many muffins does each friend get?

TIMS Task ⑤ₓ⑦

Students can use counters or paper circles to help solve the problems.

1. $24 \div 6 = 4$ muffins
2. $24 \div 4 = 6$ muffins
3. $21 \div 6 = 3$ R3 or $3\frac{1}{2}$ muffins

Student Questions	Teacher Notes

Q Marathon Mark

Mark is training for the Chicago Marathon in October. He can run 7 miles in one hour. How far will he run in 4 hours?

The marathon is 26.2 miles long. Will he be able to finish in 4 hours?

TIMS Bit $\boxed{\frac{5}{\times 7}}$

In 4 hours Mark can run 28 miles.

Students can skip count by sevens or use repeated addition.

Yes, Mark will be able to run the marathon in under four hours.

R More Base-Ten Pieces

1. Show the numbers 3042 and 3402 with base-ten pieces.

2. Show the numbers with base-ten shorthand.

3. Which number is larger? Explain how you know.

TIMS Task Ⓝ

1. 3 packs, 4 skinnies, 2 bits; 3 packs, 4 flats, 2 bits

2. □□□ |||| ··
   □□□ □□□□ ··

3. 3402 is larger because the 4 stands for 4 flats or 400; the 4 in 3042 stands for 40.

This is a review of the place value concepts the students worked on in Units 4 and 6.

S Play Digits: Largest Difference

Draw boxes on your paper like these:

□ □ □
– □ □ □
───────

As your teacher or classmate reads the digits, place them in the boxes. Try to find the largest difference. Remember each digit will only be read once.

TIMS Bit Ⓝ ✖

The directions for Digits are in Unit 6 Lesson 8. Discuss the strategies students used to place the digits as they were called.

Student Questions	Teacher Notes

(T) Cars

In one day 36,910 people bought cars in the United States. Women bought 16,241 of these cars. How many men bought cars?

TIMS Task

$$\begin{array}{r} 36{,}910 \\ -\ 16{,}241 \\ \hline 20{,}669 \text{ men} \end{array}$$

(U) Subtraction Facts Quiz A

Students take *Subtraction Facts Quiz A*, which corresponds to *Subtraction Flash Cards: Groups 1* and *2.* Then students update their *Subtraction Facts I Know* charts.

TIMS Bit

Subtraction Facts Quiz A is at the end of this set of DPP items, following item V. Ask students to have two pens or pencils of different colors ready. During the first minute of the quiz, they should write their answers using one color pen or pencil. After a minute passes, tell students to write their answers with the other color pen or pencil. Give students a reasonable time to complete the rest of the problems, then they should check their work.

3	6	9	6	2	9
5	4	9	2	9	3
9	7	8	4	7	5

(V) Twins and Triplets

On an average day in America 217 sets of twins and 5 sets of triplets are born. How many babies is this?

TIMS Task

$217 + 217 = 434$ twins

$3 \times 5 = 15$ triplets

$434 + 15 = 449$ babies

Subtraction Facts Quiz A

You will need two pens or pencils of different colors. Use the first color when you begin the test. When your teacher tells you to switch pens or pencils, finish the test using the second color.

13 − 10	15 − 9	13 − 4	16 − 10	11 − 9	19 − 10
15 − 10	13 − 9	15 − 6	12 − 10	14 − 5	12 − 9
16 − 7	17 − 10	17 − 9	14 − 10	16 − 9	14 − 9

Teacher: These facts correspond with *Subtraction Flash Cards: Groups 1* and *2*.

Lesson 1

Lemonade Stand

Lesson Overview

Students use multiplication, division, and graphing to solve problems involving a lemonade recipe. The activity introduces students to making and interpreting point graphs.

Key Content

- Using patterns in data tables and graphs to solve problems.
- Making and interpreting point graphs.
- Making and interpreting bar graphs.
- Solving multiplication and division problems.

Key Vocabulary

- extrapolation
- interpolation
- point graph

Math Facts

DPP items A, B, and C provide practice with math facts.

Homework

1. Assign the *Mr. Green's Giant Gumball Jamboree* Homework Pages in the *Discovery Assignment Book*.
2. Students study the subtraction facts in Group 1 at home using their flash cards.

Assessment

Use *Mr. Green's Giant Gumball Jamboree* Activity Pages and the *Observational Assessment Record* to note students' abilities to make and interpret point graphs.

Curriculum Sequence

Before This Unit

In *Math Trailblazers,* students have had considerable experience graphing data using bar graphs. In Grade 3 they created bar graphs in Units 1, 2, 3, and 5.

After This Unit

Students will make and interpret point graphs in Units 9, 15, and 20.

Materials List

Supplies and Copies

Student	Teacher
Supplies for Each Student • ruler	**Supplies** • lemons, sugar, water, paper cups, and a pitcher to make and serve lemonade, optional
Copies • 1 copy of *Two-column Data Table* per student (*Unit Resource Guide* Page 37) • 2 copies of *Centimeter Graph Paper* per student (*Unit Resource Guide* Page 38) • 1 copy of *Subtraction Flash Cards: Group 1* per student copied back to back, optional (*Unit Resource Guide* Pages 39–40)	**Copies/Transparencies** • 1 transparency of *Lemonade Stand Graph* (*Unit Resource Guide* Page 41) • 1 transparency of *What Went Wrong?* (*Unit Resource Guide* Page 42) • 1 copy of *Observational Assessment Record* to be used throughout this unit (*Unit Resource Guide* Pages 13–14)

All blackline masters including assessment, transparency, and DPP masters are also on the Teacher Resource CD.

Student Books

Lemonade Stand (*Student Guide* Pages 82–85)
Mr. Green's Giant Gumball Jamboree (*Discovery Assignment Book* Pages 115–118)

Daily Practice and Problems and Home Practice

DPP items A–D (*Unit Resource Guide* Pages 16–17)

Note: Classrooms whose pacing differs significantly from the suggested pacing of the units should use the Math Facts Calendar in Section 4 of the *Facts Resource Guide* to ensure students receive the complete math facts program.

Assessment Tools

Observational Assessment Record (*Unit Resource Guide* Pages 13–14)

Daily Practice and Problems

Suggestions for using the DPPs are on page 34.

A. Bit: Subtraction Facts: Group 1
(URG p. 16)

Do the following problems in your head. Write only the answers.

1. $12 - 10 =$
2. $13 - 10 =$
3. $15 - 10 =$
4. $12 - 9 =$
5. $13 - 9 =$
6. $15 - 9 =$
7. $19 - 10 =$
8. $13 - 4 =$
9. $15 - 6 =$

B. Task: Story Solving (URG p. 16)

1. Write a story and draw a picture about 8×7. Write a number sentence on your picture.
2. Write a story and draw a picture about 8×4. Write a number sentence on your picture.

C. Bit: Subtraction Flash Cards: Group 1
(URG p. 17)

1. With a partner, sort the *Subtraction Flash Cards: Group 1* into three stacks: Facts I Know Quickly, Facts I Know Using a Strategy, and Facts I Need to Learn.
2. Update your *Subtraction Facts I Know* chart. Circle the facts you answered quickly. Underline those you know by using a strategy. Do nothing to those you still need to learn.

D. Task: Messy Student (URG p. 17)

A messy student spilled some ink on a math paper. These problems got ink on them. Can you figure out the numbers that got covered up?

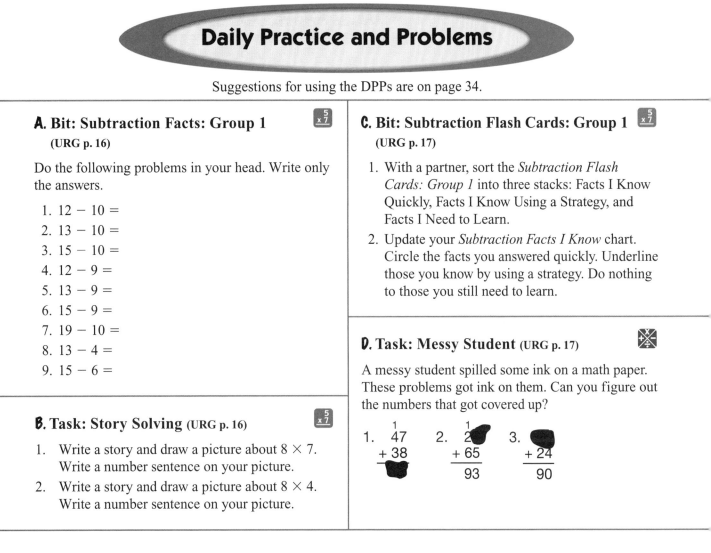

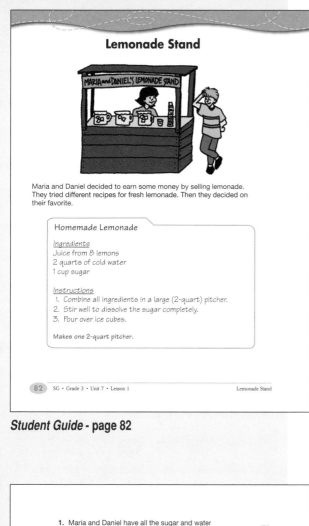

Lemonade Stand

Maria and Daniel decided to earn some money by selling lemonade. They tried different recipes for fresh lemonade. Then they decided on their favorite.

Homemade Lemonade

Ingredients
Juice from 8 lemons
2 quarts of cold water
1 cup sugar

Instructions
1. Combine all ingredients in a large (2-quart) pitcher.
2. Stir well to dissolve the sugar completely.
3. Pour over ice cubes.

Makes one 2-quart pitcher.

Student Guide - page 82

---

1. Maria and Daniel have all the sugar and water they need, but they have to buy lemons. Make a table like the one below. Use the recipe to fill in the missing data. What patterns do you see in your data table?

P Number of Pitchers	L Number of Lemons
1	
2	
4	
8	

2. Make a bar graph of the data. Number the horizontal axis by ones to at least 12. Number the vertical axis by fours to at least 80. What patterns do you see on your graph?

3. How many lemons do Maria and Daniel need to make six pitchers of lemonade? Explain how you found your answer.

A bar graph is a good way to make a picture of your data. Scientists and mathematicians also use point graphs.

4. To change your bar graph to a point graph, make a big dot at the top of each bar. Do your dots form a pattern?

5. Can you use your ruler to draw a line through the dots? Try it. Draw your line to the end of the graph in both directions.

Student Guide - page 83 *(Answers on p. 43)*

Part 1 Drawing a Bar Graph

Read the recipe for homemade lemonade on the *Lemonade Stand* Activity Pages in the *Student Guide.* Maria and Daniel face a problem: They need to know how many lemons to buy for the number of pitchers of lemonade they plan to sell. Discuss with students how to determine the number of lemons Daniel will need, and make a list of some problem-solving strategies they could use to solve the problem. This list might include using trial and error ("guess and check"), computation with or without a calculator, a data table, and a diagram.

Say:

• *Write a story and draw a picture about the number of lemons Maria and Daniel will need to make four pitchers of lemonade.*

Maria and Daniel chose to use a data table to work on their problem. See Figure 3. *Questions 1–3* guide students through the use of the data table and resulting bar graph. This early investigation of the data with a bar graph will lead to studying patterns in the data with a point graph.

P Number of Pitchers	L Number of Lemons
1	8
2	16
4	32
8	64

Figure 3: *A completed data table for* Lemonade Stand

After completing the table, students are asked to look for patterns in the data. These patterns reflect the multiplicative structure of the problem. Discussing these patterns gives students an opportunity to use words that describe multiplication. The columns in the data table reveal that the number of lemons doubles as the number of pitchers doubles. The rows in the data table show that the number of lemons is eight times the number of pitchers. These patterns can also be represented in a graph. Since students will later convert this bar graph to a point graph, check that their graphs are correctly labeled and scaled, as shown in Figure 4 and on the *Lemonade Stand Graph* Transparency Master. Look for the following:

• Are the axes scaled appropriately?

• Are the lines, rather than the spaces, numbered?

- Is each axis labeled with the name of the variable and a letter to stand for the variable?
- Do the bars lie on the vertical lines rather than between them?
- Did students use a ruler to draw the sides of each bar?
- Are the bars the correct height?
- Are the bars on the correct lines?

When they have completed their graphs, ask:

- *Describe the graph. What patterns do you see?* (Students may notice that each bar is twice as tall as the bar before it and that the bars look like steps on a stairway.)

To answer **Question 3** students often sketch the bar for six pitchers, making its height midway between the bar for four pitchers and the bar for eight pitchers. They can also add the height of the bar for four pitchers to the height of the bar for two pitchers. Using these or other methods, students should find that Maria and Daniel will need 48 lemons for six pitchers of lemonade.

Part 2 Making a Point Graph

A class discussion of student strategies for solving **Question 3** might include the observation that it is possible to fit a ruler along the tops of the bars and draw a straight line. This line can then be used to predict the height of the bar for six pitchers. **Questions 4** and **5** develop this technique.

As shown in Figure 5, students draw dots at the top of each bar and then look to see whether the dots form a pattern. Since the dots lie along a straight line, they draw a line through these points with a ruler, extending the line in both directions. You can demonstrate the procedure using a ruler and the *Lemonade Stand Graph* Transparency Master.

If the dots on the bars cannot be connected by a straight line with a ruler, the student has drawn the graph incorrectly. Use the *Lemonade Stand Graph* Transparency Master and the prompts in Part 1 to help students check the accuracy of their graphs.

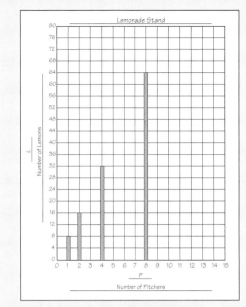

Figure 4: *A completed bar graph for* Lemonade Stand

TIMS Tip

Students will use the line to make predictions. They should therefore use rulers to make the lines as accurate as possible.

Content Note

Using this method to draw a line graph is the precursor to graphing ordered pairs. The dot at the top of the bar for 4 pitchers should lie on the grid line for 32 lemons. Students can learn, based on this experience, to graph the point (4, 32) without a lengthy explanation of ordered pairs.

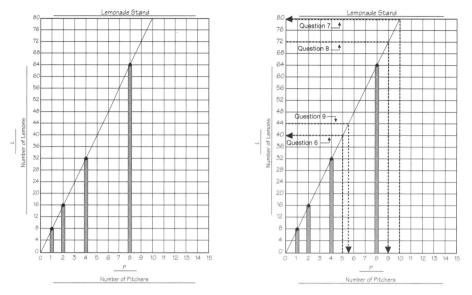

Figure 5: *Converting to a point graph and using it to interpolate and extrapolate*

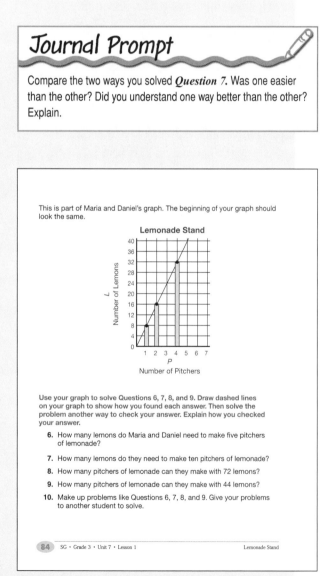

Journal Prompt

Compare the two ways you solved *Question 7.* Was one easier than the other? Did you understand one way better than the other? Explain.

This is part of Maria and Daniel's graph. The beginning of your graph should look the same.

Lemonade Stand

Use your graph to solve Questions 6, 7, 8, and 9. Draw dashed lines on your graph to show how you found each answer. Then solve the problem another way to check your answer. Explain how you checked your answer.

6. How many lemons do Maria and Daniel need to make five pitchers of lemonade?

7. How many lemons do they need to make ten pitchers of lemonade?

8. How many pitchers of lemonade can they make with 72 lemons?

9. How many pitchers of lemonade can they make with 44 lemons?

10. Make up problems like Questions 6, 7, 8, and 9. Give your problems to another student to solve.

Student Guide - page 84 *(Answers on p. 43)*

Part 3 Using the Graph to Solve Problems

In *Questions 6* and *7* students use the graph and a ruler to find the answer by drawing a line going up from the number on the horizontal axis (number of pitchers) until they reach their graph line, then extend this line left until they reach the vertical axis (number of lemons), as shown in Figure 5. Students should draw dashed lines to show their work so these lines will not be confused with the line connecting the data points. Demonstrate this on the Transparency Master. *Questions 8* and *9* will require students to perform this process in reverse: They will begin drawing their dashed line at the vertical axis (number of lemons) and will find their answer on the horizontal axis (number of pitchers).

Solving *Questions 6–9* two ways encourages students to look back at their work and discover the connection between the line graph and multiplication and division. They can solve *Questions 6* and *7* using multiplication, and *Question 8* using division. They can also solve *Question 9* using division, but this requires dealing with remainders. Since the answer is halfway between five and six, students might say Maria and Daniel can make $5\frac{1}{2}$ pitchers or they can make 5 pitchers and will have four lemons left over. Both answers are correct.

Questions 11–13 deal with the notions of cost, price, and profit. *Question 12* is an open-ended and challenging question, which can lead to lively class discussions. This question asks students to determine the price of one serving of lemonade. The explanations for how they decided on a price are important. Encourage students to share their reasoning and problem-solving strategies. Before students work on these problems, you may want to define and discuss the term *profit*.

Part 4 What Went Wrong?

Use the *What Went Wrong?* Transparency Master to help students identify errors on a graph, then look for errors on their own graphs. Compare the correct graph drawn on the *Lemonade Stand Graph* transparency to the incorrect graph on the *What Went Wrong?* transparency as you use the following discussion prompts.

- *What can you tell me about the graph?*
- *What do you see that is correct?* (the title, the label on the vertical axis)
- *What errors do you see?*
- *Are the labels on the axes correct?* (No, they are both the same. The horizontal axis should read Number of Pitchers.)
- *Are the scales correct?* (The numbers are correct, but the student labeled the spaces, not the lines on the horizontal axis. The lines are not labeled correctly on the vertical axis.)
- *Are the bars on the correct lines?* (Yes.)
- *Are the bars the correct height?* (It is difficult to tell since the vertical axis is numbered incorrectly, but the bar for two pitchers is too short and the bar for four pitchers is too tall.)
- *Did the student use a ruler to draw the line?* (No.)
- *Did the student find the number of lemons for five pitchers of lemonade correctly?* (No. The line showing his or her work does not meet the graph line.)
- *Did the student find the number of pitchers for 72 lemons correctly?* (Yes, if the axes had been scaled correctly.)

Use the discussion of the two transparency masters to develop, with your students, a checklist for making a point graph. Students may use the checklist when completing *Mr. Green's Giant Gumball Jamboree* Homework Pages and when they encounter other graphing tasks. Include questions in the checklist similar to those listed in this Lesson Guide.

Use this chart to help you solve Questions 11, 12, and 13. Explain how you found your answers.

Ingredient	Cost
Lemons	50¢ each
Sugar	25¢ per cup
Paper Cup	3¢ each
Water	free

One pitcher of lemonade makes 8 servings.

11. How much does it cost to make and sell one pitcher of lemonade?

12. What should be the price of one serving of lemonade?

13. If Maria and Daniel use this price, how much lemonade do they need to sell to make a $2 profit?

Lemonade Stand   SG • Grade 3 • Unit 7 • Lesson 1   85

Student Guide - page 85 *(Answers on p. 44)*

Content Note

Using the graph to find data points that lie between those in your data table is called **interpolation.** *Inter* means "between" or "among." Since we have data for four pitchers and eight pitchers, using the graph to answer *Question 6* (five pitchers) is interpolating. Using the graph to make predictions about data points that lie outside those in your data table is called **extrapolation.** *Extra* means "outside" or "beyond." Since 72 lemons lie beyond the largest number of lemons reported in the data table, using the graph to answer *Question 8* is extrapolating.

Name _____ Date _____

Mr. Green's Giant Gumball Jamboree

Mr. Green sells giant gumballs for 20¢ each.
Finish Mr. Green's data table of prices.

N Number of Gumballs	C Cents
1	
3	
5	
	140
9	

1. Explain how you figured out what to put in the data table. What patterns do you see in the data table?

_____
_____
_____
_____

Lemonade Stand   DAB • Grade 3 • Unit 7 • Lesson 1 **115**

Discovery Assignment Book - page 115 (Answers on p. 44)

Name _____ Date _____

2. Make a point graph of your data. Use the graph paper following Question 9.
   A. Finish numbering the axes.
   B. Label the axes.
   C. Title your graph.
3. Do the points form a pattern? If so, describe the pattern.

   _____
   _____

4. Can you use a ruler to draw a line through the points? Try it.

   Solve Questions 5, 6, 7, and 8 in two ways. First, use your graph, showing your work with dotted lines. Then solve the problem another way to check your answer. (You can also solve the problem without the graph and use the graph to check.) Explain how you found your answers.

5. How much will 4 gumballs cost?

   _____
   _____
   _____
   _____
   _____

6. How many gumballs can you buy with $1.20? (Remember: $1.20 = 120¢)

   _____
   _____
   _____
   _____
   _____

116 DAB • Grade 3 • Unit 7 • Lesson 1   Lemonade Stand

Discovery Assignment Book - page 116 (Answers on p. 45)

Math Facts

DPP items A and C provide practice with subtraction facts in Group 1. Task B asks students to draw a picture and write a story about a multiplication fact.

Homework and Practice

- Assign *Mr. Green's Giant Gumball Jamboree* Homework Pages in the *Discovery Assignment Book.* Students fill in a data table and make a point graph as they did in the *Lemonade Stand* Activity Pages. Since the data table and graph involve relatively new concepts, students may complete one or both before taking the assignment home.

- DPP Task D provides practice with addition using paper and pencil.

- Students take home *Subtraction Flash Cards: Group 1* and the list of facts they need to study, so they can practice with a family member.

Assessment

- Use the following points to assess students' problem-solving and communication skills as you read their responses to **Question 1** of *Mr. Green's Giant Gumball Jamboree.*

  1. Can students clearly describe the patterns they find?

  2. Do they use appropriate math language such as *odd numbers, multiply by 20,* or *40 cents more than?*

  3. Do they connect the patterns in this data table to any others they have seen before?

  4. Do they generalize about how to extend the pattern?

- You can use the graph in *Mr. Green's Giant Gumball Jamboree* Homework Pages to assess graphing skills. Record your observations on the *Observational Assessment Record.*

  1. Did students number and label the axes, title the graph, plot the points, and draw the line correctly?

  2. Did students use dotted lines to show the answers to the interpolation and extrapolation problems?

Make lemonade with your class using the recipe for the activity. The class uses information provided for *Questions 11–13* to determine the number of pitchers of lemonade needed to serve one cup to each class member. They then can calculate the number of lemons needed or use the graph they constructed to interpolate or extrapolate the answer.

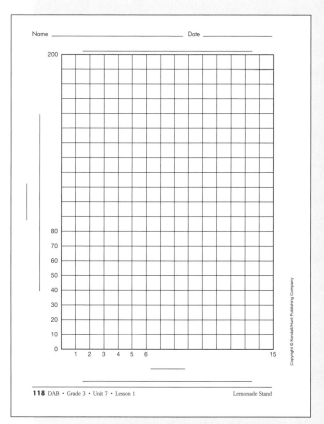

Name _____ Date _____

7. How much will 10 gumballs cost?

8. How many gumballs can you buy with $1.50?

9. How much will 24 gumballs cost? Explain how you found your answer.

Lemonade Stand   DAB • Grade 3 • Unit 7 • Lesson 1 **117**

Discovery Assignment Book - page 117 *(Answers on p. 45)*

Name _____ Date _____

118 DAB • Grade 3 • Unit 7 • Lesson 1   Lemonade Stand

Discovery Assignment Book - page 118

At a Glance

Math Facts and Daily Practice and Problems

DPP items A, B, and C provide practice with math facts. Item D provides computation practice.

Part 1. Drawing a Bar Graph

1. Students read the recipe for lemonade that is on the *Lemonade Stand* Activity Pages in the *Student Guide.*
2. Students write a story and draw a picture about the number of lemons Maria and Daniel will need to make four pitchers of lemonade.
3. Students complete *Questions 1–3,* which guide them through the use of the data table to make a bar graph.
4. Students discuss patterns in the data and use words that describe multiplication.
5. Check that students' bar graphs are correctly labeled and scaled and that bars are drawn accurately.

Part 2. Making a Point Graph

1. By completing *Questions 4–5* on the *Lemonade Stand* Activity Pages, students change their bar graphs to point graphs.
2. Demonstrate the procedure using the *Lemonade Stand Graph* Transparency Master.

Part 3. Using the Graph to Solve Problems

1. Students use their graphs to solve problems involving multiplication and division *(Questions 6–9).*
2. Students complete *Questions 10–13* and share their answers and solution strategies.

Part 4. What Went Wrong?

1. Display and discuss the *What Went Wrong?* Transparency Master.
2. With your students, develop a checklist for making a point graph.

Homework

1. Assign the *Mr. Green's Giant Gumball Jamboree* Homework Pages in the *Discovery Assignment Book.*
2. Students study the subtraction facts in Group 1 at home using their flash cards.

Assessment

Use *Mr. Green's Giant Gumball Jamboree* and the *Observational Assessment Record* to note students' abilities to make and interpret point graphs.

Extension

Make lemonade with your class using the recipe for the activity. Then have students determine the number of pitchers or lemons needed to serve one glass of lemonade to each class member.

Answer Key is on pages 43–45.

Notes:

Name _____ Date _____

_____

Name _____ Date _____

Centimeter Graph Paper, Blackline Master

$\begin{array}{r} 12 \\ -\ 9 \\ \hline \end{array}$	$\begin{array}{r} 12 \\ -10 \\ \hline \end{array}$	$\begin{array}{r} 13 \\ -\ 9 \\ \hline \end{array}$
Group 1	Group 1	Group 1
$\begin{array}{r} 13 \\ -10 \\ \hline \end{array}$	$\begin{array}{r} 13 \\ -\ 4 \\ \hline \end{array}$	$\begin{array}{r} 15 \\ -\ 9 \\ \hline \end{array}$
Group 1	Group 1	Group 1
$\begin{array}{r} 15 \\ -10 \\ \hline \end{array}$	$\begin{array}{r} 15 \\ -\ 6 \\ \hline \end{array}$	$\begin{array}{r} 19 \\ -10 \\ \hline \end{array}$
Group 1	Group 1	Group 1

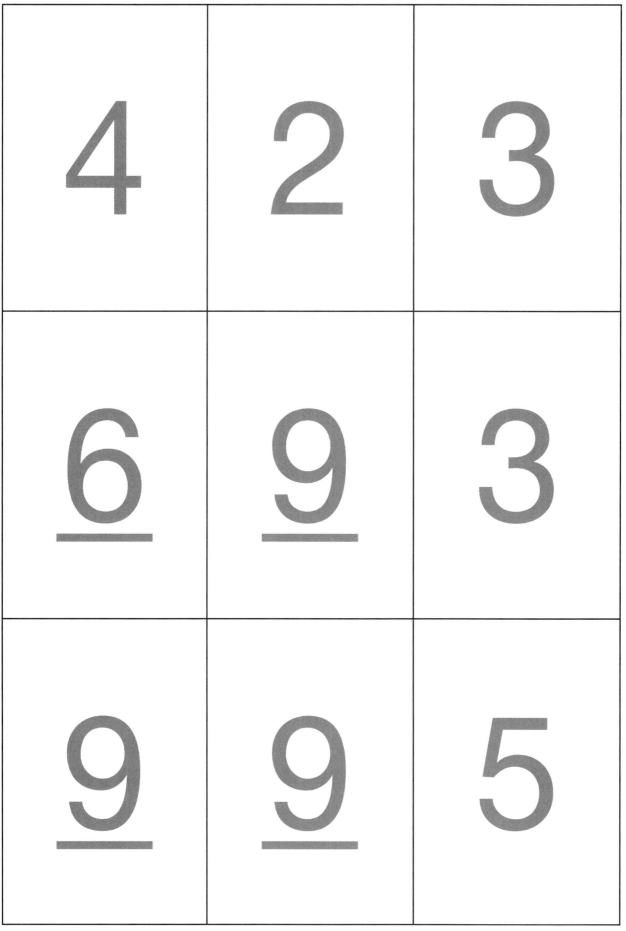

Subtraction Flash Cards: Group 1—Reverse Side

Lemonade Stand Graph

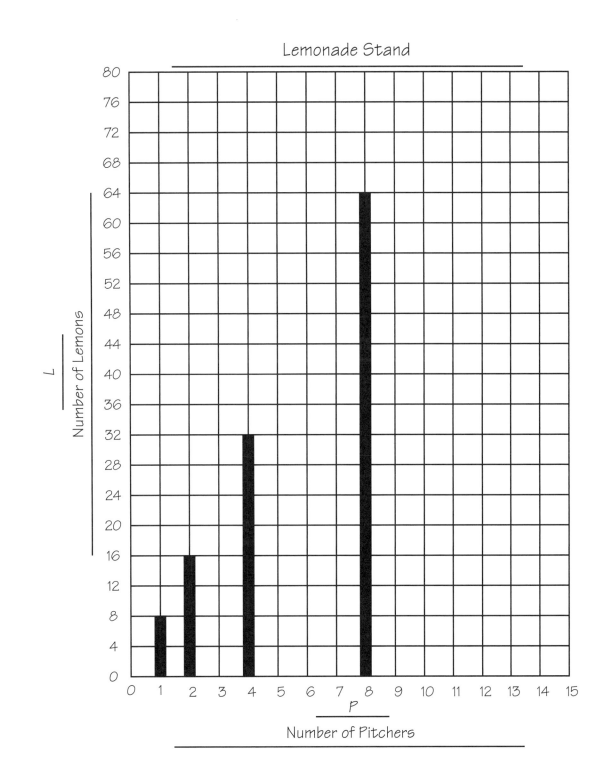

What Went Wrong?

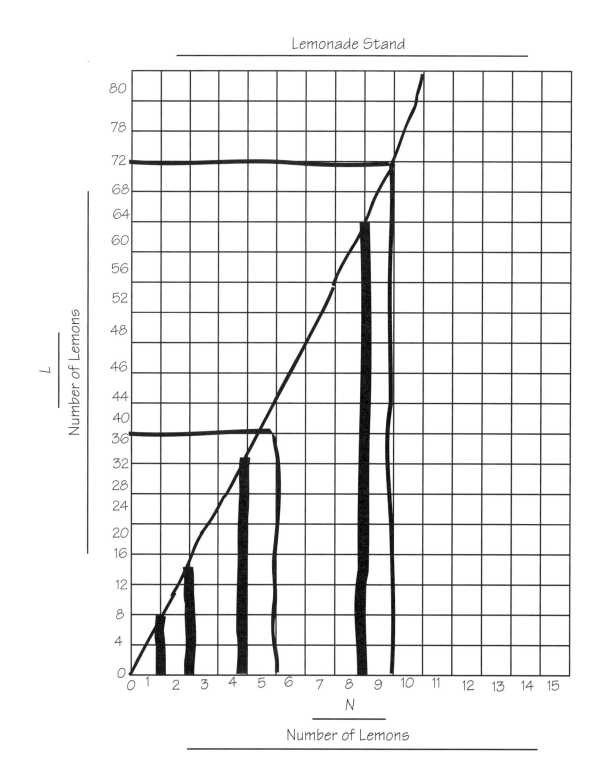

Lemonade Stand

L / Number of Lemons

N
Number of Lemons

Student Guide (p. 83)

Questions 1–13*

1. See Figure 3 in the Lesson Guide for a completed data table. Possible patterns: When the number of pitchers doubles, the number of lemons doubles. The number of lemons is the number of pitchers times 8.

2. See Figure 4 in the Lesson Guide for a completed bar graph. Possible patterns: Each bar is twice as tall as the bar before it or the bars look like stairs.

3. 48 lemons; strategies will vary. See the Lesson Guide.

For *Questions 4–9,* see Figure 5 in the Lesson Guide.

4. Yes. They appear to lie on a straight line.

5. Yes.

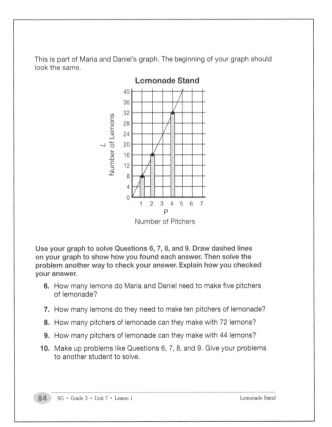

1. Maria and Daniel have all the sugar and water they need, but they have to buy lemons. Make a table like the one below. Use the recipe to fill in the missing data. What patterns do you see in your data table?

P Number of Pitchers	L Number of Lemons
1	
2	
4	
8	

2. Make a bar graph of the data. Number the horizontal axis by ones to at least 12. Number the vertical axis by fours to at least 80. What patterns do you see on your graph?

3. How many lemons do Maria and Daniel need to make six pitchers of lemonade? Explain how you found your answer.

A bar graph is a good way to make a picture of your data. Scientists and mathematicians also use point graphs.

4. To change your bar graph to a point graph, make a big dot at the top of each bar. Do your dots form a pattern?

5. Can you use your ruler to draw a line through the dots? Try it. Draw your line to the end of the graph in both directions.

Lemonade Stand   SG • Grade 3 • Unit 7 • Lesson 1   83

Student Guide - page 83

Student Guide (p. 84)

For *Questions 6–9,* solutions using interpolation and extrapolation on the graph are shown in Figure 5 in the Lesson Guide. The answer and one of many alternative solutions is given below.

6. 40 lemons; $8 + 8 + 8 + 8 + 8 = 40$ lemons

7. 80 lemons; $10 \times 8 = 80$ lemons

8. 9 pitchers; $? \times 8 = 72$; $? = 9$ pitchers of lemonade

9. Draw a picture of 44 lemons divided into 5 groups of 8 lemons and one group of 4 lemons, which gives a solution of 5 pitchers with 4 lemons left over. Or, since 4 is half of 8, an alternative solution is $5\frac{1}{2}$ pitchers.

10. One possible problem: How many lemons do we need to make 3 pitchers of lemonade?

This is part of Maria and Daniel's graph. The beginning of your graph should look the same.

Lemonade Stand

(graph: *L* Number of Lemons vs. *P* Number of Pitchers)

Use your graph to solve Questions 6, 7, 8, and 9. Draw dashed lines on your graph to show how you found each answer. Then solve the problem another way to check your answer. Explain how you checked your answer.

6. How many lemons do Maria and Daniel need to make five pitchers of lemonade?

7. How many lemons do they need to make ten pitchers of lemonade?

8. How many pitchers of lemonade can they make with 72 lemons?

9. How many pitchers of lemonade can they make with 44 lemons?

10. Make up problems like Questions 6, 7, 8, and 9. Give your problems to another student to solve.

84   SG • Grade 3 • Unit 7 • Lesson 1   Lemonade Stand

Student Guide - page 84

*Answers and/or discussion are included in the Lesson Guide.

Use this chart to help you solve Questions 11, 12, and 13. Explain how you found your answers.

Ingredient	Cost
Lemons	50¢ each
Sugar	25¢ per cup
Paper Cup	3¢ each
Water	free

One pitcher of lemonade makes 8 servings.

11. How much does it cost to make and sell one pitcher of lemonade?

12. What should be the price of one serving of lemonade?

13. If Maria and Daniel use this price, how much lemonade do they need to sell to make a $2 profit?

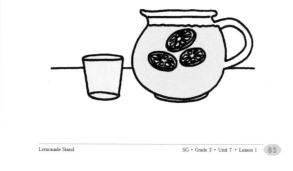

Lemonade Stand   SG • Grade 3 • Unit 7 • Lesson 1   **85**

Student Guide - page 85

Student Guide (p. 85)

11. Using a calculator: $8 \times 50¢ + 25¢ + 8 \times 3¢ = 449¢ = \$4.49$

12. Answers will vary. One serving of lemonade costs between 56¢ and 57¢ to make, so the price must be at least 58¢ to make a profit.

13. Answers will vary depending on the price the student chooses. For example, if Maria and Daniel choose to charge 75¢ a serving, the profit for one glass of lemonade is $75¢ - 56¢ = 19¢$. They will need to sell 11 servings of lemonade to make a $2 profit ($10 \times .19 = \$1.90$ and $11 \times .19 = \$2.09$).

Name _____ Date _____

Mr. Green's Giant Gumball Jamboree

Mr. Green sells giant gumballs for 20¢ each. Finish Mr. Green's data table of prices.

N Number of Gumballs	C Cents
1	
3	
5	
	140
9	

I. Explain how you figured out what to put in the data table. What patterns do you see in the data table?

_____
_____
_____
_____

Lemonade Stand   DAB • Grade 3 • Unit 7 • Lesson 1 **115**

Discovery Assignment Book - page 115

Discovery Assignment Book (p. 115)

Mr. Green's Giant Gumball Jamboree

N Number of Gumballs	C Cents
1	20
3	60
5	100
7	140
9	180

I. Students can fill in the data table by using a calculator or following patterns. Possible patterns include: The number of gumballs are the odd numbers. The cost of the gumballs always ends in zero. The cost of the gumballs increases by 40¢ for each row.*

*Answers and/or discussion are included in the Lesson Guide.

Discovery Assignment Book (p. 116)

2.

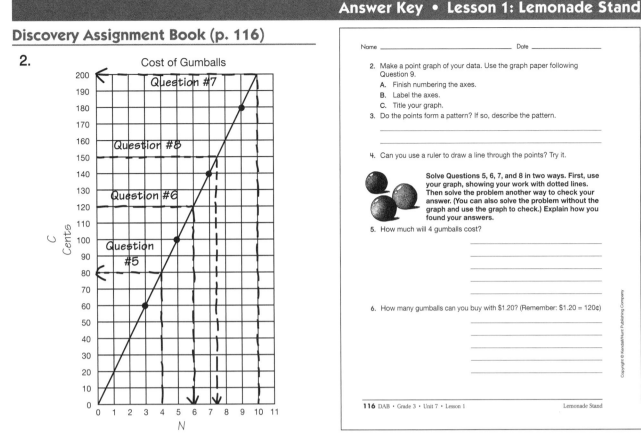

Cost of Gumballs

C Cents (vertical axis)

N Number of Gumballs (horizontal axis)

3. Yes. Possible patterns: The dots fall on a line. The dots are on stair steps.

4. See graph.

For **Questions 5–8,** interpolation and extrapolation are shown on the preceding graph. One of many alternative solutions for each problem is shown below.

5. 80¢; $4 \times 20¢ = 80¢$

6. Using the calculator: Since $20¢ + 20¢ + 20¢ + 20¢ + 20¢ + 20¢ = \$1.20$, you can buy 6 gumballs.

Discovery Assignment Book (p. 117)

7. $10 \times 20¢ = 200¢ = \$2.00$

8. 7 gumballs; since you can buy 6 gumballs with $1.20, 7 gumballs would cost $1.40. A dime is left over.

9. Using a calculator: $24 \times 20¢ = 480¢ = \$4.80$

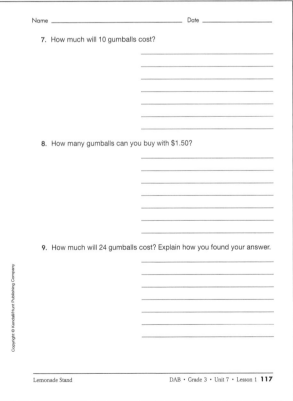

Discovery Assignment Book - page 116

Name _____ Date _____

2. Make a point graph of your data. Use the graph paper following Question 9.
   A. Finish numbering the axes.
   B. Label the axes.
   C. Title your graph.
3. Do the points form a pattern? If so, describe the pattern.
   _____
   _____
4. Can you use a ruler to draw a line through the points? Try it.

Solve Questions 5, 6, 7, and 8 in two ways. First, use your graph, showing your work with dotted lines. Then solve the problem another way to check your answer. (You can also solve the problem without the graph and use the graph to check.) Explain how you found your answers.

5. How much will 4 gumballs cost?

6. How many gumballs can you buy with $1.20? (Remember: $1.20 = 120¢)

116 DAB • Grade 3 • Unit 7 • Lesson 1   Lemonade Stand

Discovery Assignment Book - page 117

Name _____ Date _____

7. How much will 10 gumballs cost?

8. How many gumballs can you buy with $1.50?

9. How much will 24 gumballs cost? Explain how you found your answer.

Lemonade Stand   DAB • Grade 3 • Unit 7 • Lesson 1 117

Lesson 2

Katie's Job

Lesson Overview

Estimated Class Sessions
1-2

In this assessment activity, students work individually or in groups to solve problems using a graph. They look for patterns in the graph and use the graph and other strategies to solve problems.

Key Content

- Using patterns in data tables and graphs to solve problems.
- Solving multiplication and division problems.
- Communicating problem-solving strategies.

Math Facts

Task F provides computation and facts practice.

Homework

Assign Parts 1 and 2 of the Home Practice.

Assessment

1. Score student work using the Telling dimension of the *TIMS Multidimensional Rubric*.
2. Add the completed work to student portfolios.

Curriculum Sequence

Before This Unit

The Student Rubric: *Knowing* was introduced in Unit 2 Lesson 6. *Solving* was introduced in Unit 5 Lesson 5.

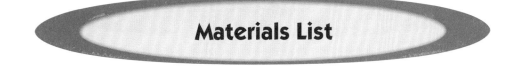

Materials List

Supplies and Copies

Student	Teacher
Supplies for Each Student • calculator • ruler	**Supplies**

Copies
 	
• 1 copy of *Katie's Job* per student
  (*Unit Resource Guide* Pages 53–54)
	Copies/Transparencies
	
	• 1 transparency of *Katie's Job*, optional
	  (*Unit Resource Guide* Pages 53–54)
	
	• 1 transparency or poster of TIMS Student Rubric:
	  Telling, optional
	  (*Teacher Implementation Guide*, Assessment section)

All blackline masters including assessment, transparency, and DPP masters are also on the Teacher Resource CD.

Student Books
Student Rubric: *Telling* (*Student Guide* Appendix C and Inside Back Cover)

Daily Practice and Problems and Home Practice
DPP items E–F (*Unit Resource Guide* Pages 17–18)
Home Practice Parts 1–2 (*Discovery Assignment Book* Page 112)

Note: Classrooms whose pacing differs significantly from the suggested pacing of the units should use the Math Facts Calendar in Section 4 of the *Facts Resource Guide* to ensure students receive the complete math facts program.

Assessment Tools
TIMS Multidimensional Rubric (*Teacher Implementation Guide*, Assessment section)

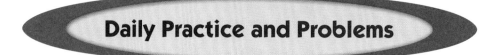

Daily Practice and Problems

Suggestions for using the DPPs are on page 51.

E. Bit: Calculator Counting by 20s
    (URG p. 17)

Work with a partner. One partner counts. The other times the counting partner. Then, switch jobs and count again.

Predict how long it will take to count by 20s to 1000. Use a calculator to count by 20s to 1000. Say the numbers quietly to yourself. How long did it take?

F. Task: Candy Bars (URG p. 18)

1. Mr. Green sells candy bars for 60¢ each. How much will 8 candy bars cost?
2. Marge spent $4.20 on candy bars at Mr. Green's store. How many candy bars did she buy?

Teaching the Activity

Students may work individually or in groups to solve the problems. Introduce the assessment by reading the paragraph at the top of the first *Katie's Job* Assessment Page. For **Question 1,** students use the graph to determine how much money Katie makes in one week. For the remaining questions, students solve the problems in two ways as they did in the previous lesson *Lemonade Stand.* In addition to using the graph, problem-solving strategies might include: trial and error, computation with or without a calculator, data tables, and diagrams. Students' explanations of their problem-solving strategies are an important part of this assessment.

Introduce the Student Rubric: *Telling,* the third and last Student Rubric. Post the *Telling* Student Rubric on a bulletin board to remind students to use it. Discuss the rubric with students. You may use this activity to review the *Knowing* and *Solving* Student Rubrics as well. Make your expectations clear by informing students the dimensions you will use to evaluate their work. As students are working, encourage them to use the Student Rubric: *Telling* to help them clearly communicate their problem-solving strategies.

Before you determine final scores for the assignment, comment on the first drafts and allow students to revise their work based on your comments. Remind students to use the Student Rubric: *Telling* as a guide in their revisions. As a class, talk about the criteria outlined in this rubric and apply it to several pieces of sample work. (You may wish to use one or more of the rubrics.) Spend time discussing how the work does or does not reflect the goals defined in the rubric. This kind of discussion helps students learn how to apply the rubric and enables them to extend their communication skills.

Student Rubric: *Telling*

What does this rubric tell you?

It helps me talk and write about math and solving problems!

In My Best Work in Mathematics:

- I show all of the steps that I used to solve the problem. I also tell what each number refers to (such as 15 boys or 6 inches).

- I explain why I solved the problem the way I did so that someone can see why my method makes sense.

- If I use tools like pictures, tables, graphs, or number sentences, I explain how the tools I used fit the problem.

- I use math words and symbols correctly. For example, if I see "6 – 2," I solve the problem "six minus two," not "two minus six."

SG • Grade 3 • Appendix C **305**

***Student Guide* - Appendix C**

Use the following questions, along with the *TIMS Multidimensional Rubric,* to guide your evaluation of students' content knowledge, problem-solving abilities, and communication skills.

Knowing

- Did students use the graph correctly to find how much Katie made in one week?
- Did students use the graph and other strategies to solve **Problems 2–5?**
- If a number sentence was used to solve the problem, did students use numbers and symbols appropriately?
- Did students calculate correctly?
- Did students interpret remainders appropriately? In **Problem 4** students may divide $50 by $12 and say that the answer is 4 weeks with $2 more to be earned. Based on their explanations, appropriate answers include $4\frac{1}{2}$ weeks, 5 weeks, and between 4 and 5 weeks.

Solving

- Did students use more than one strategy to solve each problem? For example, for **Problem 4** did students use the graph and another strategy such as division?
- Did students use the graph and other tools, such as calculators and tables, to solve the problems?
- Did students vary their strategies when solving each problem a second way?
- Did students persist in the problem-solving process until they found more than one way to solve the problem?
- Did students look back and check their answers by comparing their two solutions?

Telling

- Did students communicate their strategies for solving the problems effectively? For example, if students used the graph, did they show lines on it to indicate how they solved the problem?
- Did students explain how they handled the remainder in **Problem 4?**
- Did students communicate how they found their solutions by recording a number sentence or describing their process in words?
- Did students explain how they used the graph or other tools such as data tables or calculators to solve the problems?

Samples of student work for **Problem 4** show varying levels of communication skills. The scores reflect our ratings according to the *TIMS Multidimensional Rubric.*

Colleen's graph:

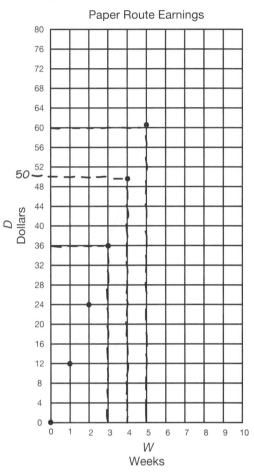

Colleen's explanation:

4 weeks and a day

Katie will have to work about 4 weeks because there are 4 12s in 48

$$12\overline{)50}$$

with quotient 4 and subtraction of 48 leaving remainder 2

Figure 6: *Colleen's explanation for* **Problem 4**

Telling, 4

Colleen showed her work on the graph. She answered the question with a clear sentence using both words and numbers. Although her interpretation of the remainder is not completely correct, we know what she did. This should result in a lower score on the Knowing dimension, but not the Telling dimension.

Marta's explanation:

I divided forty-eight by twelve and got four remainder of two. so its better to have to more than to little so I said she would have the work five weeks.

$$50 \div 12 = 4 \text{ R } 2$$

Figure 7: *Marta's explanation is logical but somewhat vague*

Telling, 3

Marta didn't show her work on the graph. Although her thinking is logical, she has some difficulty communicating clearly. Her number sentence is correct, but she used 48 instead of 50 in her explanation.

David's answer:

Four weeks.

Telling, 1

Although David provided an answer, it is unclear how he solved this problem. He provided no explanation and did not show his work on the graph.

You may want to place this assessment activity in students' portfolios. Compare students' work on this activity with previous work scored on the rubric, such as *Spinning Differences* from Unit 2 Lesson 6 and *Joe the Goldfish* from Unit 5 Lesson 5, and with future work.

Math Facts

Task F provides computation practice using multiplication facts.

Homework and Practice

- DPP Bit E builds number sense by skip counting on the calculator.
- Assign Parts 1 and 2 of the Home Practice in the *Discovery Assignment Book*. They provide practice with computation.

Answers for Parts 1 and 2 of the Home Practice are in the Answer Key at the end of this lesson and at the end of this unit.

Assessment

Use the Telling dimension of the *TIMS Multidimensional Rubric* to score *Katie's Job* Assessment Pages. Students' work from this assignment is appropriate for students' portfolios.

Name _____ Date _____

Unit 7 **Home Practice**

PART 1

1. A. 12 + 8 + 5 = _____   2. A. 100 – 90 = _____
   B. 17 + 3 + 5 = _____   B. 110 – 90 = _____
   C. 5 + 16 + 4 = _____   C. 150 – 90 = _____

3. Sara said that she used the addition facts strategy "making a ten" to solve Questions 1A–1C. Explain how you could "make a ten" to solve each problem.

_____

_____

_____

PART 2

1. A. 160 – 90 = _____   2. A. 160 + 40 = _____
   B. 160 – 100 = _____   B. 160 + 60 = _____
   C. 160 – 70 = _____   C. 160 + 80 = _____

3. Enrique and Derek bought ice cream. Together, they had $1.50. Derek bought a chocolate cone for $0.60 and Enrique bought a double-decker strawberry cone for $0.80.
   A. How much money will they have left after buying the ice cream cones? _____
   B. If they split the change evenly, how much money should each person get? _____

4. Erik wants to buy pencils at the school store. Each pencil costs 7 cents. How many pencils could he buy with 50 cents? _____ Show how you solved the problem.

112 DAB • Grade 3 • Unit 7   EXPLORING MULTIPLICATION AND DIVISION

Discovery Assignment Book - page 112 *(Answers on p. 55)*

Estimated Class Sessions **1-2**

At a Glance

Math Facts and Daily Practice and Problems

DPP Bit E builds number sense. Task F provides computation and facts practice.

Teaching the Activity

1. Present the problem described on the *Katie's Job* Assessment Pages.
2. Discuss the Student Rubric: *Telling*.
3. Individual students or teams work to solve problems. Students use the Student Rubric: *Telling* to guide their work.
4. Review the *Solving* and *Knowing* rubrics.
5. Discuss with students the criteria outlined in the Student Rubric: *Telling* dimension and apply it to several pieces of student work.
6. Comment on first drafts and give students an opportunity to revise their work.

Homework

Assign Parts 1 and 2 of the Home Practice.

Assessment

1. Score student work using the Telling dimension of the *TIMS Multidimensional Rubric.*
2. Add the completed work to student portfolios.

Answer Key is on pages 55–56.

Notes:

Name _____   Date _____

Katie's Job

Katie delivers newspapers once each week. She made this graph to help her keep track of the money she makes. You can use it to help you solve the following problems.

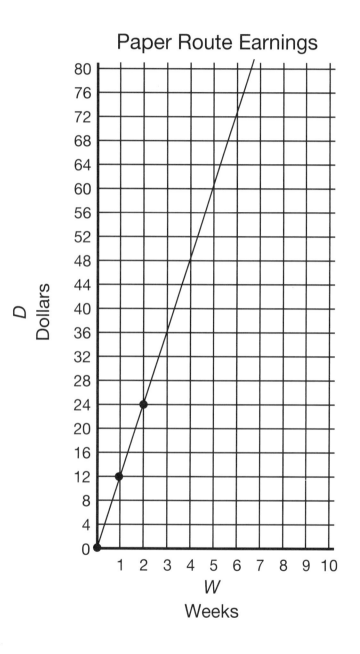

1. How much money does Katie make in one week?

_____

Solve Questions 2, 3, and 4 in two ways. First use your graph and show your work with dotted lines. Then, solve the problem another way to check your answer. (You can also solve the problem without the graph and use the graph to check.) Explain how you found your answers.

2. How much money will Katie make in five weeks?

    _____

    _____

    _____

    _____

3. If Katie wants to buy a remote-controlled car that costs $36, how many weeks will she have to save her money?

    _____

    _____

    _____

    _____

4. How many weeks will she have to work to earn $50 so she can buy a present for her mother?

    _____

    _____

    _____

    _____

5. How much money will Katie make in 12 weeks?

    _____

    _____

    _____

    _____

Discovery Assignment Book (p. 112)

Home Practice*

Part 1

  I. A. 25   **B.** 25   **C.** 25

  2. A. 10   **B.** 20   **C.** 60

  3. $(12 + 8) + 5 = 25$; $(17 + 3) + 5 = 25$; $5 + (16 + 4) = 25$; explanations will vary

Part 2

  I. A. 70   **B.** 60   **C.** 90

  2. A. 200   **B.** 220   **C.** 240

  3. A. $0.10

     B. $0.05

  4. 7 pencils; $50¢ \div 7¢ = 7$ pencils with a remainder of $1¢$; strategies will vary

Unit Resource Guide (p. 53)

Katie's Job

  I. $12

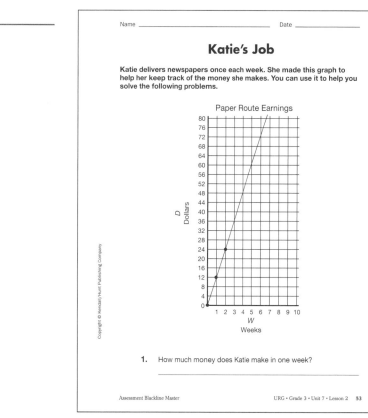

Discovery Assignment Book - page 112

Unit Resource Guide - page 53

*Answers for all the Home Practice in the *Discovery Assignment Book* are at the end of the unit.

Name _____ Date _____

Solve Questions 2, 3, and 4 in two ways. First use your graph and show your work with dotted lines. Then, solve the problem another way to check your answer. (You can also solve the problem without the graph and use the graph to check.) Explain how you found your answers.

2. How much money will Katie make in five weeks?
    _____
    _____
    _____
    _____

3. If Katie wants to buy a remote-controlled car that costs $36, how many weeks will she have to save her money?
    _____
    _____
    _____
    _____

4. How many weeks will she have to work to earn $50 so she can buy a present for her mother?
    _____
    _____
    _____
    _____

5. How much money will Katie make in 12 weeks?
    _____
    _____
    _____
    _____

54   URG • Grade 3 • Unit 7 • Lesson 2   Assessment Blackline Master

Unit Resource Guide - page 54

Unit Resource Guide (p. 54)

For *Questions 2–4* the interpolation and extrapolation are shown in the following graph. One possible alternative solution for each problem is given below.

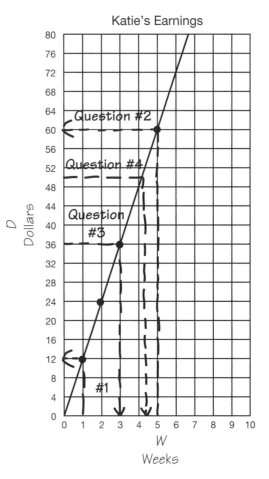

2. $5 \times \$12 = \$60$

3. 3 weeks
    $\$36 - \$12 = \$24$ (1 week)
    $\$24 - \$12 = \$12$ (2 weeks)
    $\$12 - \$12 = \$0$ (3 weeks)

4. 5 weeks. We know from *Question 3,* it takes 3 weeks to earn $36. Since $\$36 + \$12 = \$48$, it will take 4 weeks to earn $48. It will take 5 weeks to earn $60 *(Question 2)*. Katie will have $10 left over. Students might also say that the answer is between 4 and 5 weeks.

5. $144; extrapolate and find that Katie can earn $72 in 6 weeks. Katie can earn twice that amount in 12 weeks; $\$72 + \$72 = \$144$.

Lesson 3

Mathhoppers

Lesson Overview

Mathhoppers are imaginary creatures that can jump a specified number of units on a number line. Using this context, students solve problems that further their study of multiplication and division. By using repeated jumps on the number line, students can connect multiplication to repeated addition and division to repeated subtraction.

Key Content

- Representing multiplication using number lines.
- Using number lines to solve problems.
- Connecting repeated addition to multiplication.
- Connecting repeated subtraction to division.
- Writing multiplication number sentences.

Key Vocabulary

- number line

Math Facts

DPP items G and I provide practice with math facts.

Homework

1. Assign the *Professor Peabody's Mathhoppers* Homework Page.
2. Assign Part 3 of the Home Practice.
3. Students study the subtraction facts in Group 2 at home using their flash cards.

Assessment

Use the *Observational Assessment Record* to record students' abilities to represent multiplication and division using manipulatives, number lines, and words and to write number sentences for multiplication.

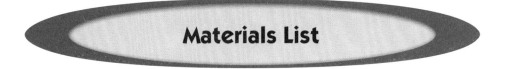

Materials List

Supplies and Copies

Student	Teacher
Supplies for Each Student • scissors • calculator • tape • centimeter connecting cubes, optional **Supplies for Each Student Group** • meterstick or measuring tape (for use as a number line) • green pattern block or other marker (for use as a mathhopper) • about 60 centimeter connecting cubes	**Supplies** • centimeter connecting cubes
Copies • 1 copy of *Subtraction Flash Cards: Group 2* per student, copied back to back, optional (*Unit Resource Guide* Pages 65–66)	**Copies/Transparencies** • 1 transparency of the first *Mathhoppers* Activity Page (*Student Guide* Page 86)

All blackline masters including assessment, transparency, and DPP masters are also on the Teacher Resource CD.

Student Books
Mathhoppers (*Student Guide* Pages 86–89)
Mathhoppers Number Line Template (*Discovery Assignment Book* Page 119)
Professor Peabody's Mathhoppers (*Discovery Assignment Book* Page 121)

Daily Practice and Problems and Home Practice
DPP items G–J (*Unit Resource Guide* Pages 18–20)
Home Practice Part 3 (*Discovery Assignment Book* Page 113)

Note: Classrooms whose pacing differs significantly from the suggested pacing of the units should use the Math Facts Calendar in Section 4 of the *Facts Resource Guide* to ensure students receive the complete math facts program.

Daily Practice and Problems

Suggestions for using the DPPs are on page 63.

G. Bit: Subtraction Facts: Group 2 $\boxed{\frac{5}{\times 7}}$
(URG p. 18)

Do the following problems in your head. Write only the answers.

1. $14 - 10 =$
2. $16 - 10 =$
3. $17 - 10 =$
4. $14 - 9 =$
5. $16 - 9 =$
6. $17 - 9 =$
7. $14 - 5 =$
8. $16 - 7 =$
9. $11 - 9 =$

H. Task: Base-Ten Pieces (URG p. 19) $\boxed{N}$

1. Show the number 3602 with base-ten pieces. Use the Fewest Pieces Rule.
2. Show this number with base-ten shorthand.

I. Bit: Subtraction Flash Cards: Group 2 $\boxed{\frac{5}{\times 7}}$
(URG p. 19)

1. With a partner, sort the *Subtraction Flash Cards: Group 2* into three stacks: Facts I Know Quickly, Facts I Know Using a Strategy, and Facts I Need to Learn.
2. Update your *Subtraction Facts I Know* chart. Circle the facts you answered quickly. Underline those you know by using a strategy. Do nothing to those you still need to learn.

J. Task: The Number 908 Is . . . . $\boxed{N}$
(URG p. 20)

The number 908 is . . .

A. 10 more than ___

B. 10 less than ___

C. 100 more than ___

D. 100 less than ___

E. about half of ___

F. about twice ___

G. $800 +$ ___

H. about $10 \times$ ___

I. $500 +$ ___

J. 110 less than ___

Mathhoppers

Mathhoppers are very special creatures. They live on number lines. Every time a mathhopper hops, it hops the same distance.

Professor Peabody studies the behavior of mathhoppers. He has found several kinds of mathhoppers. One is the +3 ("plus three") mathhopper. The +3 mathhopper always hops 3 units to the right on the number line. Professor Peabody observed a +3 mathhopper start at 0 and hop four times. Where did it land?

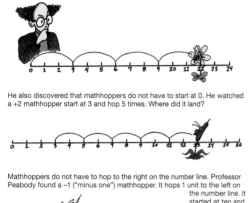

He also discovered that mathhoppers do not have to start at 0. He watched a +2 mathhopper start at 3 and hop 5 times. Where did it land?

Mathhoppers do not have to hop to the right on the number line. Professor Peabody found a –1 ("minus one") mathhopper. It hops 1 unit to the left on the number line. It started at ten and hopped 6 times. Where did it land?

Student Guide - page 86

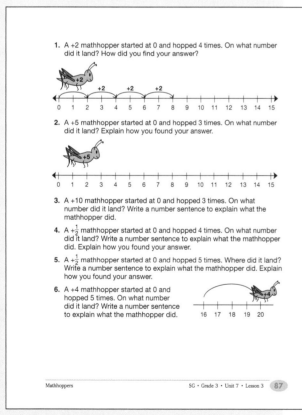

1. A +2 mathhopper started at 0 and hopped 4 times. On what number did it land? How did you find your answer?

2. A +5 mathhopper started at 0 and hopped 3 times. On what number did it land? Explain how you found your answer.

3. A +10 mathhopper started at 0 and hopped 3 times. On what number did it land? Write a number sentence to explain what the mathhopper did.

4. A $+\frac{1}{2}$ mathhopper started at 0 and hopped 4 times. On what number did it land? Write a number sentence to explain what the mathhopper did. Explain how you found your answer.

5. A $+\frac{1}{2}$ mathhopper started at 0 and hopped 5 times. Where did it land? Write a number sentence to explain what the mathhopper did. Explain how you found your answer.

6. A +4 mathhopper started at 0 and hopped 5 times. On what number did it land? Write a number sentence to explain what the mathhopper did.

Student Guide - page 87 *(Answers on p. 67)*

Teaching the Activity

Part 1   Introducing Mathhoppers

Teachers have introduced mathhoppers in several ways. One effective method is to display the transparency of the first *Mathhoppers* Activity Page in the *Student Guide* and use cubes to help students learn to visualize the mathhoppers' jumps. Students read the explanation of mathhoppers on their activity pages as you read the transparency.

Discuss the jumps that mathhoppers make. Demonstrate the first series of jumps with centimeter connecting cubes. Make four groups of three cubes to show how the +3 mathhopper hops four times. Snap each set of three cubes together individually to show one jump at a time. As you place each group of three cubes together, lay them on the first number line on the transparency as shown in Figure 8. Ask students:

- *How many hops did the +3 mathhopper make?* (4)
- *Where did the mathhopper land?* (12)

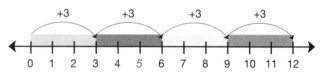

Figure 8: *Representing the hops of a +3 mathhopper using cubes on the transparency*

Demonstrate the hops of the other mathhoppers on the transparency.

You might also introduce mathhoppers by making a large number line on the floor with tape or chalk. One student can pretend to be a +3 mathhopper, beginning at zero and "hopping" four times: three, six, nine, twelve. Then, other students can give new directions to the mathhopper. For instance, they can ask him or her to be a +5 mathhopper starting at 1 and hopping 2 times.

TIMS Tip

If you work with centimeter connecting cubes, which have sides one centimeter long, you will be able to lay them along the meterstick, using it as a convenient number line.

Part 2   Mathhopper Problems

Once the class is familiar with mathhoppers, they begin working on the *Mathhoppers* Activity Pages in pairs or groups. Each group should have a number line to use when solving the problems. They can use a meterstick or tape measure as their number line and a green pattern block as a mathhopper or they can assemble their own number line using the *Mathhopper Number Line Template* Activity Page in the *Discovery Assignment Book.* Students can also sketch number lines on paper to record some of their answers. Encourage students to use a variety of number lines as they complete the problems. Some questions require a longer number line than the ones provided so students will have to solve these problems using other methods.

You can laminate the number lines assembled from the *Mathhopper Number Line Template* so they are more durable.

As students begin to solve the problems, they may need to work with manipulatives and move back and forth between manipulatives, drawings, words, and symbols. For instance, they might answer *Question 2* by connecting three groups of five cubes together. Then they could use arrows to show their answers on sketched number lines. Students can continue using this method for later questions, but they are sometimes also asked to represent a mathhopper problem as a number sentence. (Both repeated addition and multiplication sentences should be accepted.) It will not be easy for students to use cubes to help them solve *Questions 4–5* since the mathhopper is a $+\frac{1}{2}$ mathhopper. Encourage them to show half hops with arrows on number lines.

In *Questions 7–9* students must find the number of hops given the starting point, the landing point, and the size of the hops. They can use number lines and division or repeated subtraction to solve these problems. They can also use division to solve *Questions 10–11.* Students must find the size of the hops given the number of hops and the starting and ending points.

Question 12 asks students to make up two mathhopper problems for another group to solve. In checking each other's work, they should be able to resolve any discrepancies.

Write about how another group solved one of the problems you made up for *Question 12.* Was their solution different from yours? How?

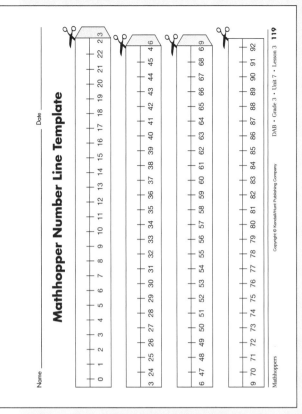

Discovery Assignment Book - page 119

7. A +4 mathhopper started at 0. It hopped until it reached 20. How many hops did it take? Explain.

8. A +2 mathhopper started at 0. It hopped until it reached 14. How many hops did it take? Explain.

9. A +8 mathhopper started at 0. It hopped until it reached 40. How many hops did it take? Explain.

10. A mathhopper started at 0 and hopped 5 times. It ended up at 20. How big were its hops? Explain.
    18 19 20

11. A mathhopper started at 0 and hopped 6 times. It landed on 60. How big were its hops? Explain.

12. Make up two mathhopper problems. Trade problems with another group. See if you can answer their problems. When they have finished answering your problems, you can check their answers.

13. Suppose we have a +5 mathhopper that started at 2. Where did it land if it hopped 3 times? Write a number sentence to explain your answer.

14. A +3 mathhopper started at 3 and hopped 6 times. Where did it land? Write a number sentence to explain what the mathhopper did.

15. A +10 mathhopper started at 3 and hopped 4 times. Where did it land? Write a number sentence to explain what the mathhopper did.

16. A +5 mathhopper started at 10 and hopped 8 times. Where did it land? Write a number sentence to explain what the mathhopper did.

Student Guide - page 88 (Answers on p. 67)

Discourage the use of number sentences such as $5 \times 2 = 10 + 3 = 13$. Since 5×2 does not equal $10 + 3$ or 13, such sentences are confusing and incorrect.

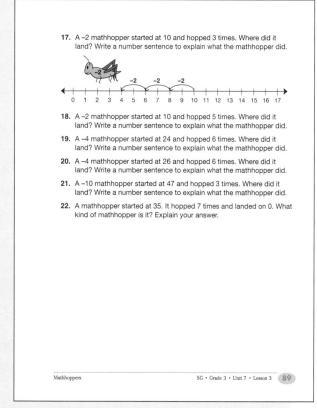

17. A –2 mathhopper started at 10 and hopped 3 times. Where did it land? Write a number sentence to explain what the mathhopper did.

18. A –2 mathhopper started at 10 and hopped 5 times. Where did it land? Write a number sentence to explain what the mathhopper did.

19. A –4 mathhopper started at 24 and hopped 6 times. Where did it land? Write a number sentence to explain what the mathhopper did.

20. A –4 mathhopper started at 26 and hopped 6 times. Where did it land? Write a number sentence to explain what the mathhopper did.

21. A –10 mathhopper started at 47 and hopped 3 times. Where did it land? Write a number sentence to explain what the mathhopper did.

22. A mathhopper started at 35. It hopped 7 times and landed on 0. What kind of mathhopper is it? Explain your answer.

Mathhoppers   SG • Grade 3 • Unit 7 • Lesson 3   89

Student Guide - page 89 *(Answers on p. 68)*

TIMS Tip

When $10 - 3 \times 2$ is input into a calculator, it may or may not show 4 as an answer. Check your calculator to see whether parentheses are needed, $10 - (3 \times 2)$.

When students report their answers during a class discussion, help them connect repeated addition to multiplication. Encourage them to use number sentences as well as appropriate multiplication and division terms in their explanations—"5 times 4" and "20 divided into groups of 4." Sharing their solutions may provide opportunities to point out the connections between the operations.

As students progress through the problems, they gain practice with new varieties of mathhoppers. *Questions 13–16* describe mathhoppers that begin hopping at numbers other than zero. Review the second mathhopper story on the transparency or first page of the activity. It asks students to write a number sentence for each problem. They may respond with a single number sentence such as $3 + 2 + 2 + 2 + 2 + 2 = 13$ or $3 + 5 \times 2 = 13$. They may also write two sentences: $5 \times 2 = 10$ and $3 + 10 = 13$.

Questions 17–22 introduce mathhoppers that hop from right to left on the number line. These "minus" hoppers all begin at numbers other than zero. Review the third mathhopper story on the transparency or first page of the activity. Encourage students to use manipulatives or number lines as they solve problems and write number sentences. Again, students might respond with a single number sentence such as $10 - 2 - 2 - 2 = 4$ or $10 - 3 \times 2 = 4$. However, they may feel more comfortable writing two sentences: $3 \times 2 = 6$ followed by $10 - 6 = 4$.

As students complete the problems on the *Mathhoppers* Activity Pages, highlight the different kinds of hops a mathhopper can make.

- "+" hops starting from zero.

  Questions 1–11 on the *Mathhoppers* Activity Pages deal with this kind of maneuver.

- "+" hops starting from numbers larger than zero.

  Questions 13–16 on the *Mathhoppers* Activity Pages deal with this kind of maneuver.

- "–" hops starting from numbers larger than zero.

  Questions 17–22 on the *Mathhoppers* Activity Pages deal with this kind of maneuver.

Math Facts

DPP Bits G and I provide practice with the subtraction facts in Group 2.

Homework and Practice

- Assign the *Professor Peabody's Mathhoppers* Homework Page in the *Discovery Assignment Book.* Students make up mathhopper problems and solve their own problems. To solve the problems at home, students can use a ruler as a number line, take cubes home from the classroom, or use drawings.

- DPP Task H reviews work with base-ten pieces. Task J builds number sense.

- Students take home *Subtraction Flash Cards: Group 2* and the list of facts they need to study, so they can practice with a family member.

- Assign Part 3 of the Home Practice.

Answers for Part 3 of the Home Practice are in the Answer Key at the end of this lesson and at the end of this unit.

Assessment

Circulate around the room as students answer **Questions 1–22** on the *Mathhoppers* Activity Pages. Note students' progress representing multiplication with different tools and their abilities to write multiplication number sentences. Record your observations on the *Observational Assessment Record.*

Extension

Use chalk to draw number lines on the playground. Then ask students to make up mathhopper problems for one another to act out.

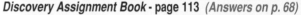

Name _____ Date _____

PART 3
Use base-ten shorthand or a shortcut method to solve the following problems. Estimate to make sure your answers are reasonable.

1. 3496
    + 707

2. 4357
    + 2828

3. 359
    − 176

4. 3001
    − 1998

5. Explain your estimation strategy for Question 4.
_____
_____
_____

PART 4
1. Shelby has $5.00 in her piggy bank. Her piggy bank only has coins inside. What coins might Shelby have that add up to $5.00? Give at least two examples.
_____

2. Jeffrey wants to visit his grandmother after his Little League game on Saturday. If his Little League game ends at 11:35 and it takes 25 minutes to travel to his grandmother's house, what time will Jeffrey begin his visit? _____ Show how you solved the problem.

EXPLORING MULTIPLICATION AND DIVISION   DAB • Grade 3 • Unit 7 **113**

Discovery Assignment Book - page 113 (Answers on p. 68)

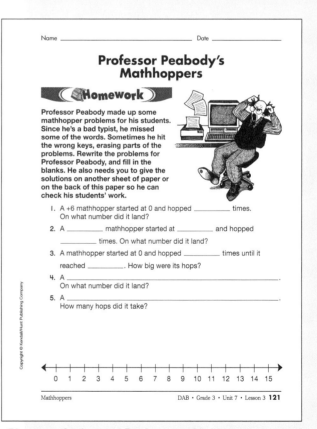

Name _____ Date _____

Professor Peabody's Mathhoppers

Homework

Professor Peabody made up some mathhopper problems for his students. Since he's a bad typist, he missed some of the words. Sometimes he hit the wrong keys, erasing parts of the problems. Rewrite the problems for Professor Peabody, and fill in the blanks. He also needs you to give the solutions on another sheet of paper or on the back of this paper so he can check his students' work.

1. A +6 mathhopper started at 0 and hopped _____ times. On what number did it land?

2. A _____ mathhopper started at _____ and hopped _____ times. On what number did it land?

3. A mathhopper started at 0 and hopped _____ times until it reached _____. How big were its hops?

4. A _____. On what number did it land?

5. A _____. How many hops did it take?

```
←─┼──┼──┼──┼──┼──┼──┼──┼──┼──┼──┼──┼──┼──┼──┼──→
  0  1  2  3  4  5  6  7  8  9 10 11 12 13 14 15
```

Mathhoppers   DAB • Grade 3 • Unit 7 • Lesson 3 **121**

Discovery Assignment Book - page 121 (Answers on p. 69)

At a Glance

Math Facts and Daily Practice and Problems

DPP items G and I provide practice with math facts. Items H and J build number sense and understanding of place value.

Part 1. Introducing Mathhoppers

1. Use a transparency of the first *Mathhoppers* Activity Page in the *Student Guide* and centimeter connecting cubes to introduce students to mathhoppers.
2. Model using connecting cubes for mathhoppers' hops.
3. (optional) Make a large number line on the floor and have students pretend they are mathhoppers making hops.

Part 2. Mathhopper Problems

1. Student groups complete the problems on the *Mathhoppers* Activity Pages.
2. Students explore using tools that can help them solve the problems: connecting cubes; metersticks; tape measures, or number lines made from the *Mathhopper Number Line Template* in the *Discovery Assignment Book*; sketches of number lines; and number sentences.
3. Students make up mathhopper problems for their peers to solve.
4. Students share their solutions to mathhopper problems.

Homework

1. Assign the *Professor Peabody's Mathhoppers* Homework Page.
2. Assign Part 3 of the Home Practice.
3. Students study the subtraction facts in Group 2 at home using their flash cards.

Assessment

Use the *Observational Assessment Record* to record students' abilities to represent multiplication and division using manipulatives, number lines, and words and to write number sentences for multiplication.

Extension

Use chalk to draw number lines on the playground. Students can act out mathhopper problems.

Answer Key is on pages 67–69.

Notes:

Name _____   Date _____

$\begin{array}{r} 14 \\ -\ 10 \\ \hline \end{array}$	$\begin{array}{r} 14 \\ -\ 9 \\ \hline \end{array}$	$\begin{array}{r} 14 \\ -\ 5 \\ \hline \end{array}$
Group 2	Group 2	Group 2
$\begin{array}{r} 17 \\ -\ 10 \\ \hline \end{array}$	$\begin{array}{r} 17 \\ -\ 9 \\ \hline \end{array}$	$\begin{array}{r} 11 \\ -\ 9 \\ \hline \end{array}$
Group 2	Group 2	Group 2
$\begin{array}{r} 16 \\ -\ 9 \\ \hline \end{array}$	$\begin{array}{r} 16 \\ -\ 7 \\ \hline \end{array}$	$\begin{array}{r} 16 \\ -\ 10 \\ \hline \end{array}$
Group 2	Group 2	Group 2

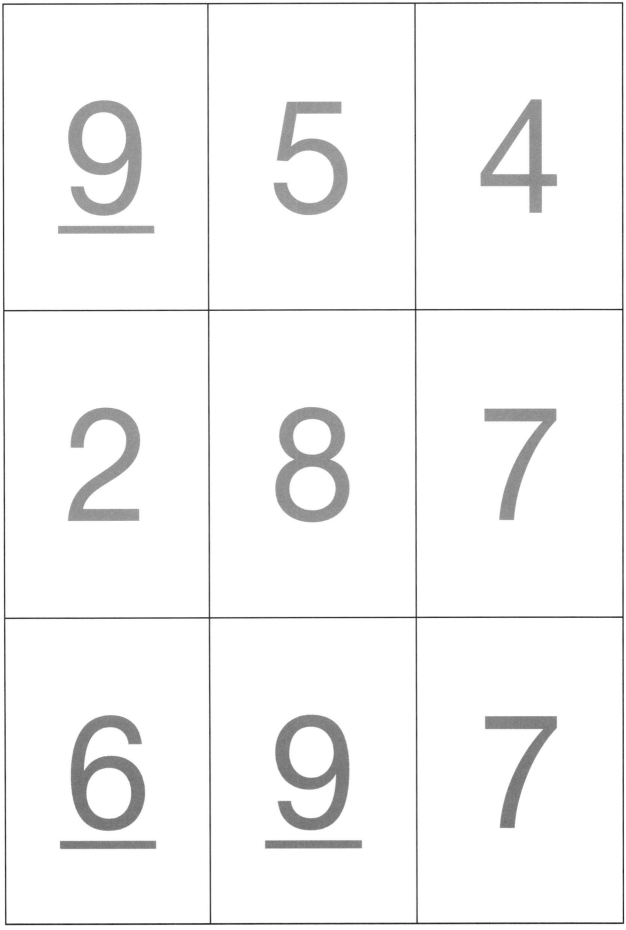

Subtraction Flash Cards: Group 2—Reverse Side

Student Guide (p. 87)

For *Questions 1–22,* number sentences may vary. We have provided one possible number sentence.*

1. $8; 2 + 2 + 2 + 2 = 8$
2. $15; 5 + 5 + 5 = 15$
3. $30; 10 + 10 + 10 = 30$
4. $2; \frac{1}{2} + \frac{1}{2} + \frac{1}{2} + \frac{1}{2} = 2$
5. $2\frac{1}{2}; \frac{1}{2} + \frac{1}{2} + \frac{1}{2} + \frac{1}{2} + \frac{1}{2} = 2\frac{1}{2}$
6. $20; 5 \times 4 = 20$

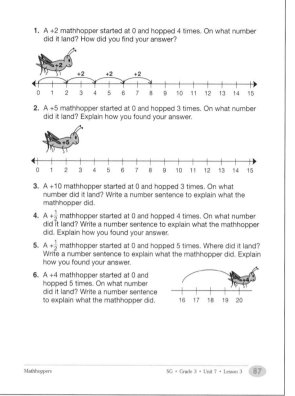

Student Guide - page 87

Student Guide (p. 88)

7. 5 hops. The number sentence in *Question 6* helps answer *Question 7.*

8. 7 hops; since $7 \times 2 = 14$, it will take a $+2$ hopper 7 hops to reach 14.

9. 5 hops; $5 \times 8 = 40$

10. 4 units. Again the number sentence in *Question 6* ($5 \times 4 = 20$) can help answer this problem.

11. 10 units; $6 \times 10 = 60$

12. Answers will vary. Look for problems such as the following: A $+6$ mathhopper hops 4 times. Where did it land?

13. 17; single number sentence:
$2 + 5 + 5 + 5 = 17$. Two sentences:
$5 \times 3 = 15; 15 + 2 = 17$

14. $21; 3 + 6 \times 3 = 21$

15. $43; 3 + 10 + 10 + 10 + 10 = 43$

16. $50; 10 + 8 \times 5 = 50$

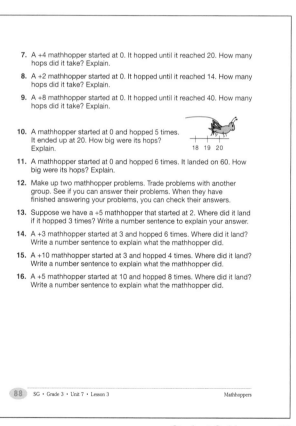

Student Guide - page 88

*Answers and/or discussion are included in the Lesson Guide.

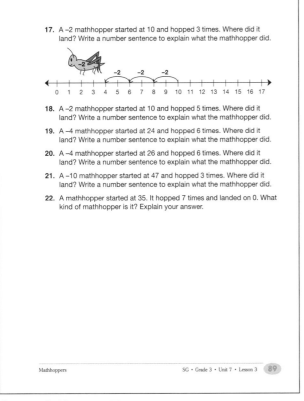

17. A −2 mathhopper started at 10 and hopped 3 times. Where did it land? Write a number sentence to explain what the mathhopper did.

18. A −2 mathhopper started at 10 and hopped 5 times. Where did it land? Write a number sentence to explain what the mathhopper did.

19. A −4 mathhopper started at 24 and hopped 6 times. Where did it land? Write a number sentence to explain what the mathhopper did.

20. A −4 mathhopper started at 26 and hopped 6 times. Where did it land? Write a number sentence to explain what the mathhopper did.

21. A −10 mathhopper started at 47 and hopped 3 times. Where did it land? Write a number sentence to explain what the mathhopper did.

22. A mathhopper started at 35. It hopped 7 times and landed on 0. What kind of mathhopper is it? Explain your answer.

Mathhoppers   SG • Grade 3 • Unit 7 • Lesson 3   89

Student Guide - page 89

Student Guide (p. 89)

17. 4; $10 - 2 - 2 - 2 = 4$

18. 0; $10 - 2 - 2 - 2 - 2 - 2 = 0$

19. 0; $24 - 6 \times 4 = 0$

20. 2; $26 - 6 \times 4 = 2$

21. 17; $47 - 10 - 10 - 10 = 17$

22. −5 mathhopper; students can use manipulatives or a number line to explain their answer.

Name _____ Date _____

PART 3
Use base-ten shorthand or a shortcut method to solve the following problems. Estimate to make sure your answers are reasonable.

1. 3496
    + 707

2. 4357
    + 2828

3.   359
    − 176

4. 3001
    − 1998

5. Explain your estimation strategy for Question 4.

_____
_____
_____

PART 4
1. Shelby has $5.00 in her piggy bank. Her piggy bank only has coins inside. What coins might Shelby have that add up to $5.00? Give at least two examples.

_____
_____

2. Jeffrey wants to visit his grandmother after his Little League game on Saturday. If his Little League game ends at 11:35 and it takes 25 minutes to travel to his grandmother's house, what time will Jeffrey begin his visit? _____ Show how you solved the problem.

EXPLORING MULTIPLICATION AND DIVISION   DAB • Grade 3 • Unit 7 **113**

Discovery Assignment Book - page 113

Discovery Assignment Book (p. 113)

Home Practice*

Part 3

1. 4203

2. 7185

3. 183

4. 1003

5. Strategies will vary. Possible strategy: $3000 - 2000 = 1000$.

---

*Answers for all the Home Practice in the *Discovery Assignment Book* are at the end of the unit.

Discovery Assignment Book (p. 121)

Professor Peabody's Mathhoppers

For *Questions 1–5,* answers will vary.

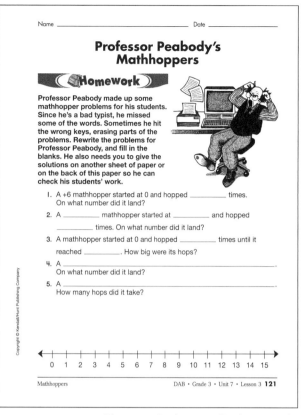

Discovery Assignment Book - page 121

Lesson 4

Birthday Party

Lesson Overview

Estimated Class Sessions

2

In the context of a birthday party, students work in groups or pairs on a set of problems they can solve using division. Using students' solutions as a foundation, lead a discussion about division and introduce division number sentences.

Key Content

- Representing multiplication using manipulatives and words.
- Solving division problems.
- Communicating problem-solving strategies.
- Interpreting remainders.
- Writing division number sentences.

Key Vocabulary

- remainder

Homework

Assign the Homework section of the *Birthday Party* Activity Pages.

Assessment

Use journal entries to assess students' abilities to communicate their solution strategies and represent multiplication and division using manipulatives, number lines, and other tools.

Materials List

Supplies and Copies

Student	Teacher
Supplies for Each Student • calculator **Supplies for Each Student Pair** • 30 or more counters	**Supplies**
Copies	**Copies/Transparencies**

All blackline masters including assessment, transparency, and DPP masters are also on the Teacher Resource CD.

Student Books
Birthday Party (*Student Guide* Pages 90–92)

Daily Practice and Problems and Home Practice
DPP items K–N (*Unit Resource Guide* Pages 20–21)

Note: Classrooms whose pacing differs significantly from the suggested pacing of the units should use the Math Facts Calendar in Section 4 of the *Facts Resource Guide* to ensure students receive the complete math facts program.

Daily Practice and Problems

Suggestions for using the DPPs are on page 74.

K. Bit: Counting by Half Hours (URG p. 20)

Count by half hours beginning with 7:00 A.M. and ending at 7:00 P.M. Begin like this:

7:00, 7:30, 8:00, 8:30, 9:00 . . .

L. Task: Time (URG p. 20)

How long have you been awake today?

How long have you been in school?

How long is it until the bell rings the next time?

M. Bit: Shortcut Addition and Subtraction (URG p. 21)

Do the following problems using a shortcut method. You may use base-ten shorthand if you wish.

1. $\begin{array}{r} 241 \\ + 83 \\ \hline \end{array}$

2. $\begin{array}{r} 517 \\ - 45 \\ \hline \end{array}$

3. $\begin{array}{r} 5479 \\ + 4067 \\ \hline \end{array}$

4. $\begin{array}{r} 4005 \\ - 3975 \\ \hline \end{array}$

5. Explain a way to do Question 4 using mental math.

N. Task: Triangles, Hexagons, and Pentagons (URG p. 21)

Here is a regular triangle, a regular hexagon, and a regular pentagon. In a regular shape, all the sides are the same length and all the angles are equal.

Draw a triangle that is not a regular triangle.

Draw a hexagon that is not a regular hexagon.

Draw a pentagon that is not a regular pentagon.

Teaching the Activity

Students work in pairs to solve problems on the *Birthday Party* Activity Pages in the *Student Guide.* Each problem focuses on how Tina will divide various items for her birthday party. Although students can solve the problems using division, they may use a variety of strategies to arrive at the answer.

Give each pair about thirty counters. Encourage students to use them to solve the problems and to provide explanations with words and pictures. If students answer the questions without the counters, ask them to use the counters to check their solutions.

As students work, help them describe what they are doing by rephrasing the problem. For example, *Question 1* can be restated as:

• *How many groups of 4 are in 15?*

Journal Prompt

Show as many different ways to solve *Question 1* as you can.

Pay special attention to the way students deal with remainders. Although 15 ÷ 4 = 3 with 3 left over, it would be impolite for Tina to let three guests stand. In this case, the answer must be four tables. *Question 5* asks students to decide how to share thirty cupcakes equally among twelve people. Clearly, each person can eat two cupcakes, but students must decide what to do with the six leftover cupcakes. They can choose to note the number left or they can divide each of the six leftover cupcakes in half so that each person gets $2\frac{1}{2}$ cupcakes.

Question 6, unlike the other problems, deals with fractions when it asks how much pizza each of twelve people can eat if they order six pizzas. Have students draw pictures to represent the problem, as they did in Unit 3 Lesson 3 *Multiplication Stories.*

Discuss students' solutions, strategies, and explanations with the class. As appropriate, introduce division notation during this discussion. The use of division symbols is one way to represent the solution, but not the only way. Also, point out the possible variations for each problem. For example, the appropriate division sentence for *Question 5* depends on how students deal with the remainder. If they divide the leftover cupcakes in half, the number sentence is 30 ÷ 12 = $2\frac{1}{2}$ cupcakes. If students report six cupcakes left over, the number sentence is 30 ÷ 12 = 2 R6. Point out that the "R" in this problem stands for **remainder,** or the number left over.

Student Guide - page 90 (Answers on p. 76)

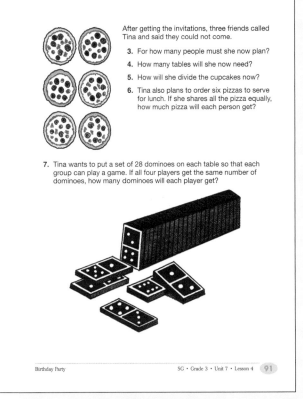

Student Guide - page 91 (Answers on p. 76)

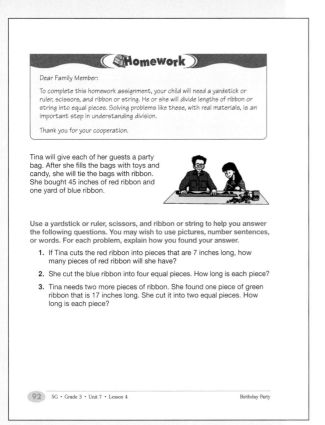

Student Guide - page 92 *(Answers on p. 77)*

When students use a calculator to solve division problems, they will often see decimals in the display. If they are confused by the answer on the calculator, ask them to solve the problem a different way and to compare the results. For example, if students use the calculator to solve *Question 1,* they will enter $15 \div 4$ and the display will read 3.75. If they solve the problem using manipulatives, they will find that the number of card tables Tina needs for 15 guests is four, since $15 \div 4 = 3$ R3.

For now, students can use the whole number to the left of the decimal and need only understand that digits to the right of the decimal indicate that there is a remainder. They can interpret the remainder based on the context of the problem. Using calculators with this activity can add the topic of decimals to a discussion about interpreting remainders.

Content Note

Division sentences can be written in many ways, each of which provides different information to the reader. During these early experiences with division, we write sentences like the example on the far left below. The next two examples are important in understanding fractions and decimals and will be introduced later in the curriculum. In *Math Trailblazers* we use the representation of division on the far right below infrequently in third grade, but students should be aware that others use this notation.

$$27 \div 6 = 4 \text{ R3} \qquad 27 \div 6 = 4.5 \quad \frac{27}{6} = 4\frac{1}{2} \qquad 6\overline{)27}^{\,4\text{ R3}}$$

Homework and Practice

- Assign the Homework section on the *Birthday Party* Activity Pages in the *Student Guide.* To complete the assignment, students must know that one yard is equal to thirty-six inches.

- DPP items K and L involve elapsed time. Bit M provides computation practice. Task N introduces regular polygons.

Assessment

Read students' written work to assess their abilities to communicate strategies. Check to see whether students use pictures and number sentences and describe the use of manipulatives with appropriate mathematical terms.

Math Facts and Daily Practice and Problems

DPP items K and L involve elapsed time. Bit M is computation practice, and Task N is a geometry problem.

Teaching the Activity

1. Student pairs complete the problems on the *Birthday Party* Activity Pages in the *Student Guide* using a variety of strategies and manipulatives.
2. Introduce division number sentences as one way to represent solutions.
3. Discuss interpreting remainders—when it is appropriate to cut up the leftovers (cupcakes) and when it is appropriate to round up (children at a table).
4. Discuss how remainders appear on calculators.

Homework

Assign the Homework section of the *Birthday Party* Activity Pages.

Assessment

Use journal entries to assess students' abilities to communicate their solution strategies and represent multiplication and division using manipulatives, number lines, and other tools.

Answer Key is on pages 76–77.

Notes:

Student Guide - page 90

Student Guide (p. 90)

Birthday Party

Note: Explanations will vary. Encourage the use of manipulatives and number sentences. One possible number sentence is given in the answers below.

1. 4 tables*

2. 2 cupcakes; $30 \div 15 = 2$ cupcakes

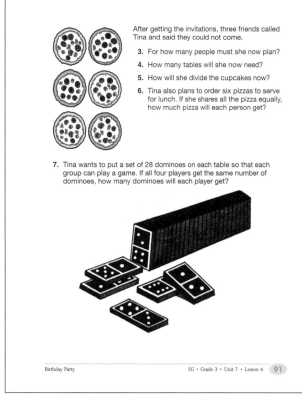

Student Guide - page 91

Student Guide (p. 91)

3. 12 people; $15 - 3 = 12$ people

4. 3 tables; $4 + 4 + 4 = 12$ people

5. 2 cupcakes for each guest with 6 cupcakes left over or $2\frac{1}{2}$ cupcakes; $30 \div 12 = 2\frac{1}{2}$*

6. $\frac{1}{2}$ pizza*

7. 7 dominoes; $7 + 7 + 7 + 7 = 28$ dominoes

*Answers and/or discussion are included in the Lesson Guide.

Student Guide (p. 92)

Homework

Note: Number sentences may vary. One possible number sentence is given in the answers below.

1. 6 pieces of ribbon with 3 inches left over; $7 \times 6 = 42; 42 + 3 = 45$

2. 9 inches; $36 \div 4 = 9$

3. $8\frac{1}{2}$ inches; $17 \div 2 = 8\frac{1}{2}$

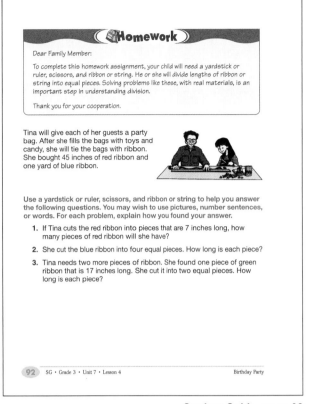

Student Guide - page 92

Lesson 5

The Money Jar

Lesson Overview

Estimated Class Sessions

1

Students solve a series of problems in which they divide money equally among the members of a family. They write number sentences to show their solutions.

Key Content

- Representing division using manipulatives.
- Solving division problems.
- Writing division number sentences.
- Solving problems involving money.

Math Facts

DPP Task P provides practice with division.

Homework

Assign the homework problems on *The Money Jar* Activity Pages.

Assessment

1. Use DPP Task P to assess students' understanding of division.
2. Use the *Observational Assessment Record* to note students' abilities to represent division using manipulatives.

Materials List

Supplies and Copies

Student	Teacher
Supplies for Each Student • play money: 60 pennies, 50 dimes, and 10 nickels • calculator • scissors, optional	**Supplies**
Copies • 1 copy of *Money Masters* per student group to substitute for play money, optional (*Unit Resource Guide* Pages 85–87)	**Copies/Transparencies**

All blackline masters including assessment, transparency, and DPP masters are also on the Teacher Resource CD.

Student Books
The Money Jar (*Student Guide* Pages 93–94)

Daily Practice and Problems and Home Practice
DPP items O–P (*Unit Resource Guide* Page 22)

Note: Classrooms whose pacing differs significantly from the suggested pacing of the units should use the Math Facts Calendar in Section 4 of the *Facts Resource Guide* to ensure students receive the complete math facts program.

Assessment Tools
Observational Assessment Record (*Unit Resource Guide* Pages 13–14)

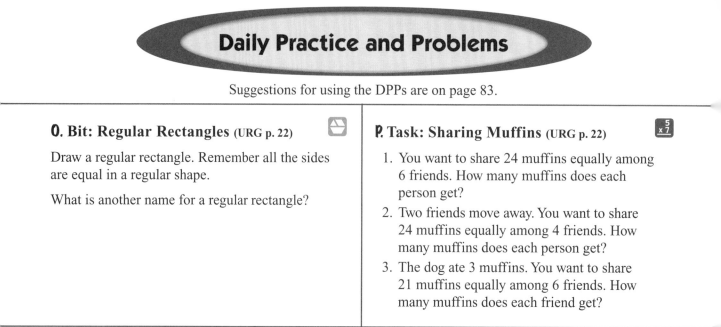

Daily Practice and Problems

Suggestions for using the DPPs are on page 83.

O. Bit: Regular Rectangles (URG p. 22)

Draw a regular rectangle. Remember all the sides are equal in a regular shape.

What is another name for a regular rectangle?

P. Task: Sharing Muffins (URG p. 22)

1. You want to share 24 muffins equally among 6 friends. How many muffins does each person get?

2. Two friends move away. You want to share 24 muffins equally among 4 friends. How many muffins does each person get?

3. The dog ate 3 muffins. You want to share 21 muffins equally among 6 friends. How many muffins does each friend get?

The ongoing activity, *Multiples on the Calendar,* introduced in Unit 3 *Exploring Multiplication,* is related to this activity. If you have used *Multiples on the Calendar* as part of your daily routine, students have practiced partitioning numbers into equal groups. This practice prepares them for solving problems with division and writing number sentences.

If play money is not available for this activity, make copies of the *Money Masters* Blackline Masters and have students cut out the coins they will need.

Read the short story about the Franklins on *The Money Jar* Activity Pages in the *Student Guide.* The Franklins save their coins in a jar. Once each month they divide the coins among the family members: The pennies are divided among the four children and the dimes are divided among the six family members. Any leftovers are returned to the jar.

Distribute the play money or a copy of the *Money Masters* Transparency Masters to each group. Encourage students to use the play money as manipulatives to solve the problems. Since there are four children in the Franklin family, form groups of four so each can act as one of the children. As students work, talk with individual groups, asking how they are solving the problems. In this way you can help them verbalize the division process.

The directions for the problems instruct students to write number sentences. More than one number sentence is possible for each problem. For example, *Question 2* requires students to divide thirty-eight pennies among four children. Students may see the problem as repeated subtraction and write their solution as shown in Figure 9.

```
    3 8
  –   4   ← 1
    3 4
  –   4   ← 2
    3 0
  –   4   ← 3
    2 6
  –   4   ← 4
    2 2
  –   4   ← 5
    1 8
  –   4   ← 6
    1 4
  –   4   ← 7
    1 0
  –   4   ← 8
      6
  –   4   ← 9
      2
```

Figure 9: *Using repeated subtraction*

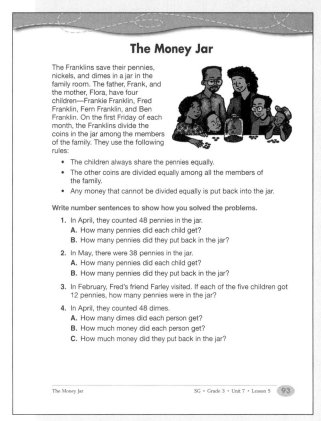

The Money Jar

The Franklins save their pennies, nickels, and dimes in a jar in the family room. The father, Frank, and the mother, Flora, have four children—Frankie Franklin, Fred Franklin, Fern Franklin, and Ben Franklin. On the first Friday of each month, the Franklins divide the coins in the jar among the members of the family. They use the following rules:

- The children always share the pennies equally.
- The other coins are divided equally among all the members of the family.
- Any money that cannot be divided equally is put back into the jar.

Write number sentences to show how you solved the problems.

1. In April, they counted 48 pennies in the jar.
   A. How many pennies did each child get?
   B. How many pennies did they put back in the jar?

2. In May, there were 38 pennies in the jar.
   A. How many pennies did each child get?
   B. How many pennies did they put back in the jar?

3. In February, Fred's friend Farley visited. If each of the five children got 12 pennies, how many pennies were in the jar?

4. In April, they counted 48 dimes.
   A. How many dimes did each person get?
   B. How much money did each person get?
   C. How much money did they put back in the jar?

The Money Jar   SG • Grade 3 • Unit 7 • Lesson 5   93

Student Guide - page 93 (Answers on p. 88)

Content Note

Classroom Management. For this activity, four seems to be the maximum number of students for a good working group. If more than four students work together, you will often see at least one student in the group who is not fully participating in the activity. Student pairs are also effective.

The following job assignments for student groups have proven successful during group problem solving:

Reader   Reads each question before the group begins solving the problem.

Checker   Makes sure each group member has a written solution to the problem before the reader reads the next problem.

Reporter   Presents the group's solution to the rest of the class. The reporter is the only member of the group who can ask the teacher questions. This forces students to ask questions of their fellow classmates before turning to the teacher for help.

Materials   Gets all the handouts, manipulatives, or
Gatherer   calculators for the group.

All students are expected to participate in the problem solving and related discussion within the group.

Students can use other combinations of addition, subtraction, and multiplication to record their solutions. During class discussion, highlight the relationships between the various sentences. For example, ask the reporter from each group to write their number sentence for **Question 2** on the board and tell the class what each number represents. For all the sentences, *38* represents the total number of pennies, *4* represents the number of children or groups, *9* represents the number of pennies in each group, and *2* represents the leftovers.

Questions 4–8 involve dimes. In **Question 4,** the family divides forty-eight dimes among six people. To determine how much money each person gets, students can use the play money to distribute the dimes equally. They should find that forty-eight dimes divided among six people means each person has eight ($48 \div 6 = 8$). Therefore, each person gets eighty cents.

To solve **Questions 5–6** students must interpret the remainders. In **Question 5** the family divides thirty-one dimes among the six members. In this case, each person gets five dimes or fifty cents, and one dime is returned to the jar. In **Question 6,** however, the remainder (thirty cents) may be returned to the jar, but another solution is also possible. After the fifteen dimes have been divided among the six members ($15 \div 6 = 2$ R3), students can trade nickels for the remaining three dimes so that each person can have two dimes and one nickel (twenty-five cents). You may need to prompt students to consider trading dimes for nickels. The two possible solutions should provoke a lively debate.

If students use calculators to solve these problems, they will be faced with the task of interpreting the results. Point out that they will get different results depending on whether they enter the number of coins or the amount of money into the calculator. The table on the left illustrates the different answers students will get and an appropriate interpretation. Experimenting with the calculator in conjunction with using the manipulatives allows students to explore the decimal representation of money.

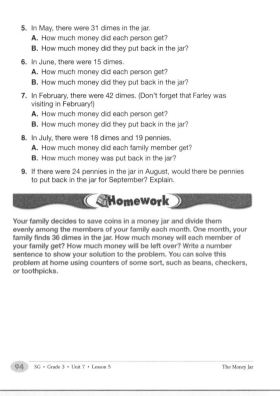

5. In May, there were 31 dimes in the jar.
   A. How much money did each person get?
   B. How much money did they put back in the jar?

6. In June, there were 15 dimes.
   A. How much money did each person get?
   B. How much money did they put back in the jar?

7. In February, there were 42 dimes. (Don't forget that Farley was visiting in February!)
   A. How much money did each person get?
   B. How much money did they put back in the jar?

8. In July, there were 18 dimes and 19 pennies.
   A. How much money did each family member get?
   B. How much money was put back in the jar?

9. If there were 24 pennies in the jar in August, would there be pennies to put back in the jar for September? Explain.

Homework

Your family decides to save coins in a money jar and divide them evenly among the members of your family each month. One month, your family finds 36 dimes in the jar. How much money will each member of your family get? How much money will be left over? Write a number sentence to show your solution to the problem. You can solve this problem at home using counters of some sort, such as beans, checkers, or toothpicks.

94   SG • Grade 3 • Unit 7 • Lesson 5   The Money Jar

Student Guide - page 94 (Answers on p. 88)

Journal Prompt

Can there be more than one right answer to a math problem? Why or why not? Give an example, and explain your answer.

Entering and Interpreting Money Problems on the Calculator

Question	Entered as Number of Coins	Entered as Dollars and Cents
4	$48 \div 6 = 8$ Give each person 8 dimes or 80¢.	$4.80 \div 6 = 0.80$ Give each person 0.80 (80¢) or 8 dimes.
5	$31 \div 6 = 5.1666666$ Give each person 5 dimes or 50¢. There are some dimes left over.	$3.10 \div 6 = 0.5166666$ Give each person 0.50 (50¢) or 5 dimes. There is something left over.
6	$15 \div 6 = 2.5$ Give each person 2 dimes or 20¢. There are some dimes left over, which can be traded for nickels, so each person gets 2 dimes and 1 nickel.	$1.50 \div 6 = 0.25$ Give each person 0.25 (25¢) or 2 dimes and 1 nickel.

82   URG • Grade 3 • Unit 7 • Lesson 5

Homework and Practice

- Assign the homework on *The Money Jar* Activity Pages.
- DPP Bit O is a question about regular shapes.

Assessment

- Use DPP Task P to assess students' progress in solving division problems and writing number sentences.
- Use the *Observational Assessment Record* to note students' abilities to represent division using manipulatives.

Literature Connection

- Silverstein, Shel. "Smart." In *Where the Sidewalk Ends,* p. 35. HarperCollins Children's Books, New York, 1974.

In this poem, a young boy thinks he is smart because he trades his dollar bill for two quarters "cause two is more than one," he trades his two quarters for three dimes because "three is more than two," and so on. Lead a class discussion that begins with the question:

"Was the boy in the poem smart to trade his dollar for coins?"

Compare the value and number of the coins in each trade.

At a Glance

Math Facts and Daily Practice and Problems

DPP Bit O is a geometry problem. Task P provides practice with division.

Teaching the Activity

1. Read the story about the Franklins on *The Money Jar* Activity Pages in the *Student Guide.*
2. Pass out scissors and the *Money Masters* Blackline Masters for students to cut out paper coins to use as manipulatives or distribute play money.
3. Students work in groups of four and complete the problems on *The Money Jar* Activity Pages.
4. Students share their solutions, strategies, and number sentences for the problems.
5. Students discuss the results obtained from using a calculator to interpret remainders.

Homework

Assign the homework problems on *The Money Jar* Activity Pages.

Assessment

1. Use DPP Task P to assess students' understanding of division.
2. Use the *Observational Assessment Record* to note students' abilities to represent division using manipulatives.

Connection

Read and discuss "Smart" by Shel Silverstein.

Answer Key is on page 88.

Notes:

Name _____ Date _____

Money Masters

Name _____   Date _____

Money Masters

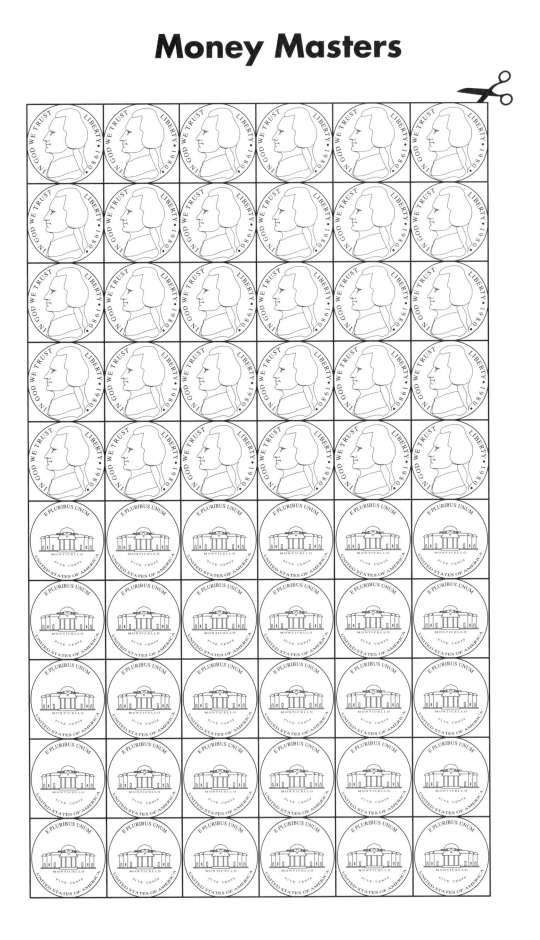

Blackline Master

Name _____ Date _____

Money Masters

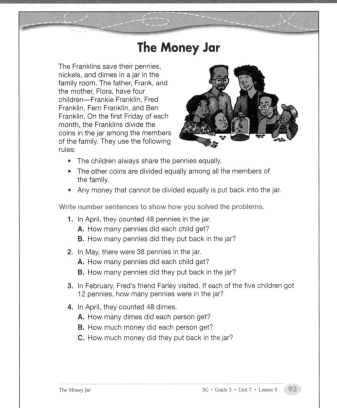

Student Guide - page 93

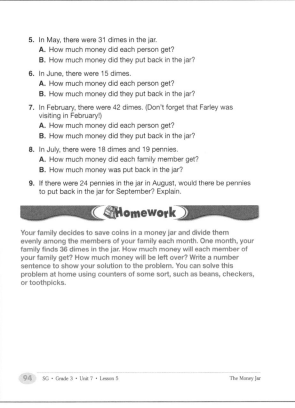

Student Guide - page 94

*Answers and/or discussion are included in the Lesson Guide.

Student Guide (p. 93)

The Money Jar*

Note: Each number sentence given is a division sentence where appropriate. Accept other number sentences such as repeated subtraction or multiplication.

1. **A.** 12 pennies; $48 \div 4 = 12$ pennies
   B. 0 pennies returned to the jar
2. **A.** 9 pennies
   B. 2 pennies returned to the jar
3. 60 pennies; $5 \times 12 = 60$ pennies
4. **A.** $48 \div 6 = 8$ dimes
   B. 8 dimes or 80¢
   C. nothing returned to the jar

Student Guide (p. 94)

5. **A.** $31 \div 6 = 5$ R1; 5 dimes or 50¢
   B. 1 dime or 10¢ returned to the jar
6. **A.** $15 \div 6 = 2$ R3; 2 dimes or 20¢
   B. 3 dimes or 30¢ returned to the jar

Or

6. **A.** 2 dimes and 1 nickel (25¢)
   B. no money returned to the jar;
   $\$1.50 \div 6 = \$0.25$
7. **A.** 6 dimes or 60¢; $42 \div 7 = 6$ dimes
   B. no money returned to the jar
8. **A.** parents—3 dimes or 30¢; children—3 dimes and 4 pennies or 34¢
   B. 3 pennies returned to the jar
9. No; $24 \div 4 = 6$ pennies for each child; no pennies returned to the jar

Lesson 6

Walking around Shapes

Estimated Class Sessions

3

Students measure the perimeter and length of one side of each of three sizes of regular polygons. They record their measurements in data tables and graph the data. They look for the relationship between the length of a side and the perimeter of equilateral triangles, squares, and regular hexagons and write multiplication and division number sentences to express these relationships. Then students use these patterns to solve problems.

Key Content

- Measuring length in centimeters.
- Measuring perimeter in centimeters.
- Identifying and describing patterns.
- Using patterns to solve problems.
- Identifying regular shapes.

Key Vocabulary

- equilateral triangle
- perimeter
- regular hexagon
- regular pentagon

Math Facts

DPP Bit Q practices math facts. Bit U is a quiz on subtraction facts.

Homework

1. Assign the *Walking around Squares* Homework Pages.
2. Assign Part 4 of the Home Practice.

Assessment

1. Students complete the *Professor Peabody's Shapes Data* Assessment Page.
2. DPP item U is a quiz on the subtraction facts in Groups 1 and 2.
3. Use the *Observational Assessment Record* to note students' abilities to find perimeter.
4. Transfer appropriate documentation from the Unit 7 *Observational Assessment Record* to students' *Individual Assessment Record Sheets*.

Materials List

Supplies and Copies

Student	Teacher
Supplies for Each Student • ruler	**Supplies**
Copies • 1 copy of *Subtraction Facts Quiz A* per student (*Unit Resource Guide* Page 25) • 1 copy of *Professor Peabody's Shapes Data* per student (*Unit Resource Guide* Page 98) • 3 copies of *Centimeter Graph Paper* per student (*Unit Resource Guide* Page 38)	**Copies/Transparencies** • 1 transparency of *Walking around Triangles* (*Discovery Assignment Book* Page 124) • 1 transparency of *Centimeter Graph Paper* (*Unit Resource Guide* Page 38)

All blackline masters including assessment, transparency, and DPP masters are also on the Teacher Resource CD.

Student Books

Student Rubric: *Telling* (*Student Guide* Appendix C and Inside Back Cover)
Walking around Shapes (*Discovery Assignment Book* Page 123)
Walking around Triangles (*Discovery Assignment Book* Page 124)
Walking around Hexagons (*Discovery Assignment Book* Pages 125–126)
Walking around Squares (*Discovery Assignment Book* Pages 127–128)

Daily Practice and Problems and Home Practice

DPP items Q–V (*Unit Resource Guide* Pages 23–24)
Home Practice Part 4 (*Discovery Assignment Book* Page 113)

Note: Classrooms whose pacing differs significantly from the suggested pacing of the units should use the Math Facts Calendar in Section 4 of the *Facts Resource Guide* to ensure students receive the complete math facts program.

Assessment Tools

Observational Assessment Record (*Unit Resource Guide* Pages 13–14)
Individual Assessment Record Sheet (*Teacher Implementation Guide,* Assessment section)

Daily Practice and Problems

Suggestions for using the DPPs are on pages 94–95.

Q. Bit: Marathon Mark (URG p. 23)

Mark is training for the Chicago Marathon in October. He can run 7 miles in one hour. How far will he run in 4 hours?

The marathon is 26.2 miles long. Will he be able to finish in 4 hours?

R. Task: More Base-Ten Pieces (URG p. 23)

1. Show the numbers 3042 and 3402 with base-ten pieces.
2. Show the numbers with base-ten shorthand.
3. Which number is larger? Explain how you know.

S. Bit: Play Digits: Largest Difference (URG p. 23)

Draw boxes on your paper like these:

☐ ☐ ☐
− ☐ ☐ ☐

As your teacher or classmate reads the digits, place them in the boxes. Try to find the largest difference. Remember each digit will only be read once.

T. Task: Cars (URG p. 24)

In one day 36,910 people bought cars in the United States. Women bought 16,241 of these cars. How many men bought cars?

U. Bit: Subtraction Facts Quiz A (URG p. 24)

Students take *Subtraction Facts Quiz A*, which corresponds to *Subtraction Flash Cards: Groups 1* and *2*. Then students update their *Subtraction Facts I Know* charts.

V. Task: Twins and Triplets (URG p. 24)

On an average day in America 217 sets of twins and 5 sets of triplets are born. How many babies is this?

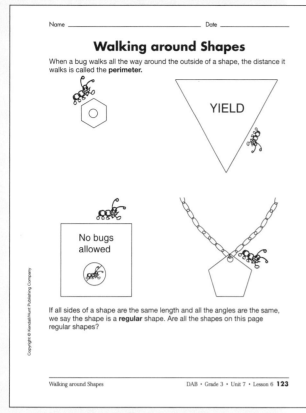

Discovery Assignment Book - page 123

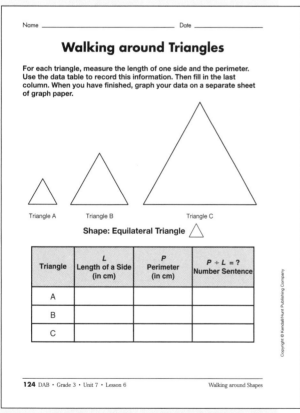

Discovery Assignment Book - page 124 *(Answers on p. 99)*

Part 1 **Walking around Triangles**

Introduce this activity with the *Walking around Shapes* Activity Page in the *Discovery Assignment Book,* which provides an opportunity to discuss the terms perimeter, equilateral triangle, and regular shape. At this point in third grade, students need to be only somewhat familiar with these terms. On the page, **perimeter** is defined as the distance a bug travels when it walks all the way around a shape. Ask students to generalize perimeter to items in the world around them, such as their desks.

An **equilateral triangle** has three sides of the same length and three angles with the same measure. Shapes are **regular** if all the sides have the same length and all the angles have the same measure. For instance, a square is a regular rectangle, and an **equilateral triangle** is also a regular triangle. You may also want to review the names of the shapes at this time.

Ask students to turn to the *Walking around Triangles* Activity Page. Instruct students to measure the perimeter and length of one side of each of the triangles. As they measure, they record the measurements in the data table.

Shape: Equilateral Triangles			
Triangle	*L* Length of a Side (in cm)	*P* Perimeter (in cm)	*P* ÷ *L* = ? Number Sentence
A	2	6	6 ÷ 2 = 3
B	4	12	12 ÷ 4 = 3
C	8	24	24 ÷ 8 = 3

Figure 10: *A filled-in data table*

Discuss the patterns and relationships in the data. See Figure 10. To facilitate discussion, pose questions similar to those that follow. A possible student response is shown after each question.

- *Do you see any patterns in the data?* (Perimeter divided by length is always three centimeters.)

- *Do you see any patterns in the columns of the data table?* (The numbers in the middle two columns double.)

- *Do you see any patterns in the rows of the data table?* (Each one is three times the other. Also, if you add the sides three times, you get the perimeter.)

- *How many sides do the triangles have? Are the sides all the same length? Do the three sides have anything to do with the pattern?* (You multiply by three because there are three equal sides. Also, perimeter divided by length is always three because there are always three sides.)

- *Can you write a number sentence that tells about the perimeter of an equilateral triangle when the length of one side is 2 centimeters? Can you write a different number sentence?* (Possible answers include $2 + 2 + 2 = 6$; $3 \times 2 = 6$; $6 \div 2 = 3$.)

- *Can you write addition, multiplication, and division sentences for this problem?* (See previous answers.)

If students need help interpreting the multiplication and division sentences, write "$6 \div 2 = 3$" (Triangle A) on the transparency and ask:

- *Why did I write the six?*
- *Where is the two in my data table?*
- *Why is the answer three?*

You can ask similar questions about the multiplication sentences. You can repeat this exercise by asking for number sentences for triangles with sides of 4 centimeters and 8 centimeters.

The next step is to model making a point graph of the data. To do this, plot the Length of the Side (L) on the horizontal axis and the Perimeter (P) on the vertical axis. The horizontal axis should be scaled by ones and the vertical axis should be scaled by twos, as indicated in Figure 11. This will allow sufficient space on the graph for extrapolation. Ask students:

- *Do the points form a pattern?*

Once they recognize that these points fall on a straight line, use a ruler to draw a line through the points, extending the line in both directions. Ask:

- *Can you use the line to find the perimeter of an equilateral triangle that has a side of 10 centimeters?* (30 cm)

Ask a student volunteer to model the extrapolation using dashed lines, as in Figure 11. Discuss other methods for finding the perimeter by asking questions similar to those used in the earlier discussion of the data table.

Part 2 Walking around Hexagons

For the second part of the activity, tell students to turn to the *Walking around Hexagons* Activity Pages, which should be completed in groups. These pages are similar to *Walking around Triangles* except students are asked to look for the relationship between the

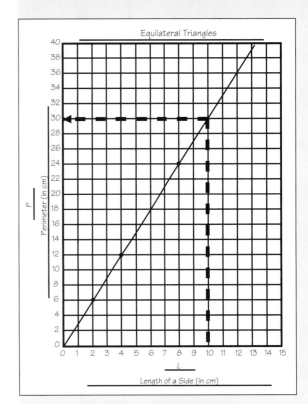

Figure 11: *Graph for* Walking around Triangles

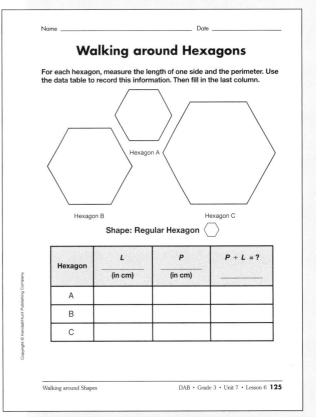

Discovery Assignment Book - page 125 *(Answers on p. 100)*

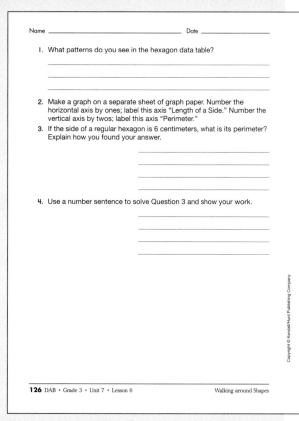

Name _____ Date _____

1. What patterns do you see in the hexagon data table?
   _____
   _____
   _____

2. Make a graph on a separate sheet of graph paper. Number the
   horizontal axis by ones; label this axis "Length of a Side." Number the
   vertical axis by twos; label this axis "Perimeter."

3. If the side of a regular hexagon is 6 centimeters, what is its perimeter?
   Explain how you found your answer.
   _____
   _____
   _____
   _____

4. Use a number sentence to solve Question 3 and show your work.
   _____
   _____
   _____
   _____

126 DAB · Grade 3 · Unit 7 · Lesson 6   Walking around Shapes

***Discovery Assignment Book* - page 126** *(Answers on p. 100)*

perimeter and length of one side of regular hexagons. They complete a data table, look for patterns in the data, make a graph of the data, and use these tools to solve problems.

For **Question 3** students can use their graphs to interpolate the perimeter of a hexagon that has a side of 6 centimeters or they can use any other method that is effective and is meaningful to them. Connect students' solutions to the graph and the number sentence in **Question 4.**

Journal Prompt

I can find the perimeter of a regular shape by …

Math Facts

DPP Bit Q provides practice with multiplication facts.

Homework and Practice

- Assign the *Walking around Squares* Homework Pages. These pages can also be used as an assessment.

- DPP Task R builds understanding of place value using base-ten shorthand. Bit S is a version of the *Digits* game. Tasks T and V are computation word problems.

- Assign Part 4 of the Home Practice as homework. It contains problems involving time and money.

Answers for Part 4 of the Home Practice are in the Answer Key at the end of this lesson and at the end of this unit.

- If *Walking around Squares* is used as an assessment, look for the following:

  1. Did the student fill in the data table correctly?

  2. Did he or she title the graph, label axes, scale the graph correctly, and plot the points correctly?

  3. Did he or she draw a line through the points with a ruler, extend the line beyond the data points, and show any interpolation with dotted lines?

- Use the *Professor Peabody's Shapes Data* Assessment Page to assess students' abilities to solve a problem about perimeter and communicate the solution. Remind students to use the Student Rubric: *Telling,* introduced in Lesson 2, to guide their work.

- DPP item U is *Subtraction Facts Quiz A.* Use it to assess students' fluency with the subtraction facts in Groups 1 and 2. Students use the results to update their *Subtraction Facts I Know* charts.

- Use the *Observational Assessment Record* to note students' abilities to find perimeter.

- Transfer appropriate documentation from the Unit 7 *Observational Assessment Record* to students' *Individual Assessment Record Sheets.*

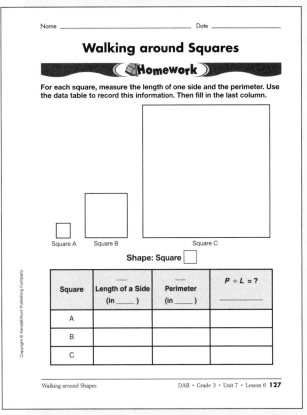

Name _____ Date _____

Walking around Squares

Homework

For each square, measure the length of one side and the perimeter. Use the data table to record this information. Then fill in the last column.

Square A   Square B   Square C

Shape: Square ☐

Square	Length of a Side (in ____)	Perimeter (in ____)	P ÷ L = ? _____
A			
B			
C			

Walking around Shapes   DAB • Grade 3 • Unit 7 • Lesson 6 **127**

Discovery Assignment Book - page 127 *(Answers on p. 101)*

Name _____ Date _____

PART 3
Use base-ten shorthand or a shortcut method to solve the following problems. Estimate to make sure your answers are reasonable.

1. 3496
    + 707

2. 4357
    + 2828

3. 359
    − 176

4. 3001
    − 1998

5. Explain your estimation strategy for Question 4.

_____
_____
_____

PART 4

1. Shelby has $5.00 in her piggy bank. Her piggy bank only has coins inside. What coins might Shelby have that add up to $5.00? Give at least two examples.

_____
_____

2. Jeffrey wants to visit his grandmother after his Little League game on Saturday. If his Little League game ends at 11:35 and it takes 25 minutes to travel to his grandmother's house, what time will Jeffrey begin his visit? _____ Show how you solved the problem.

EXPLORING MULTIPLICATION AND DIVISION   DAB • Grade 3 • Unit 7 **113**

Discovery Assignment Book - page 113 *(Answers on p. 99)*

Name _____ Date _____

1. What patterns do you see in the square data table?

_____
_____
_____

2. Make a graph on a separate sheet of graph paper. Number the horizontal axis by ones; label this axis "Length of a Side." Number the vertical axis by twos; label this axis "Perimeter."

3. What is the perimeter of a square that has a side 6 centimeters long? Explain how you found your answer, and draw the square.

_____
_____

128 DAB • Grade 3 • Unit 7 • Lesson 6   Walking around Shapes

Discovery Assignment Book - page 128 *(Answers on p. 101)*

- Look around the school for a large equilateral triangle, hexagon, or square. Measure one side, and ask students to predict the perimeter using the patterns they found in this activity. Then, measure the shape to check their predictions.

- Make a class graph with all three lines (triangles, hexagons, and squares) on the same graph and label each line with the appropriate shape. Use large graph paper or a transparency. Ask students to compare the lines as you pose the following questions:

  1. *How are the lines the same?* (They all start at (0,0) and are straight.)

  2. *How are they different?* (Some are steeper than others, and some slant more than others.)

  3. *Which is the steepest?* (The hexagons' line.)

  4. *Which is the next steepest?* (The squares' line.)

  5. *Why is the line for the hexagon the steepest?* Prompt as needed: *Which shape has the most sides?* (The hexagon has the most sides.)

  6. *Where do you think the line for octagons will appear on the graph?* (It will be even steeper than the line for the hexagons.)

  7. *Where do you think the line for pentagons will appear on the graph?* (It will be between the lines for squares and hexagons.)

At a Glance

Math Facts and Daily Practice and Problems

DPP Bit Q provides practice with math facts. Bit U is a quiz on subtraction facts. Items R and S build place value concepts. Tasks T and V are computation problems.

Part 1. Walking around Triangles

1. Discuss the terms perimeter, equilateral triangle, and regular shapes using the *Walking around Shapes* Activity Page in the *Discovery Assignment Book.*
2. Students measure the perimeter and length of one side of each of the triangles on the *Walking around Triangles* Activity Page.
3. Students record the measurements in the data table.
4. Discuss the patterns and relationships in the data table. Discuss the multiplication and division sentences.
5. Make a point graph of the data in the table on the *Walking around Triangles* Activity Pages using the transparency of *Centimeter Graph Paper.*
6. Discuss methods, such as extrapolation and multiplication, that can be used to find the perimeter of an equilateral triangle with a side length of 10 cm.

Part 2. Walking around Hexagons

1. Students work in groups to measure the perimeter and length of one side of each of the hexagons on the *Walking around Hexagons* Activity Pages.
2. Students complete a data table, look for patterns in the data, make a graph of the data, and use these tools to solve problems.

Homework

1. Assign the *Walking around Squares* Homework Pages.
2. Assign Part 4 of the Home Practice.

Assessment

1. Students complete the *Professor Peabody's Shapes Data* Assessment Page.
2. DPP item U is a quiz on the subtraction facts in Groups 1 and 2.
3. Use the *Observational Assessment Record* to note students' abilities to find perimeter.
4. Transfer appropriate documentation from the Unit 7 *Observational Assessment Record* to students' *Individual Assessment Record Sheets.*

Extension

1. Find a large equilateral triangle, hexagon, or square in the school. Measure one side and have students predict the perimeter.
2. Make a class graph with all 3 lines (triangles, hexagons, and squares). Discuss the graph.

Answer Key is on pages 99–102.

Notes:

Professor Peabody's Shapes Data

1. Professor Peabody studied the side length and the perimeter of different regular shapes. Unfortunately, he was not careful and spilled ink on one of his data tables. Help him fill in the missing data.

Shape: Regular Pentagon

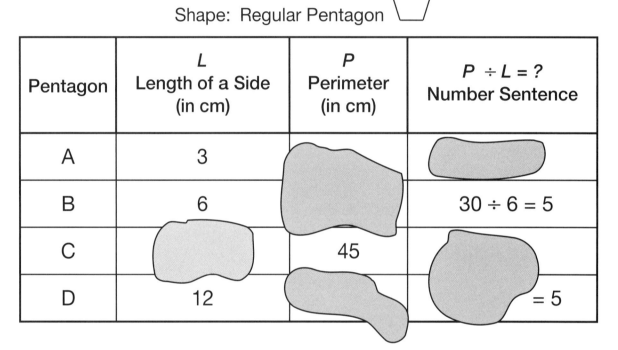

Pentagon	L Length of a Side (in cm)	P Perimeter (in cm)	$P \div L = ?$ Number Sentence
A	3		
B	6		$30 \div 6 = 5$
C		45	
D	12		$= 5$

2. A bug walked all the way around this figure so that it ended up where it started. The distance it walked is 36 centimeters. The figure is made of four identical equilateral triangles. How long is the side of each triangle? Solve the problem two ways to be sure you are right. On a separate page, explain how you found both your answers.

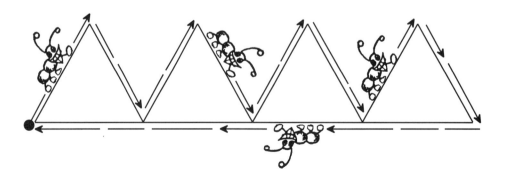

Discovery Assignment Book (p. 113)

Home Practice*

Part 4

1. Answers will vary. Any combination of coins that equal $5.00 is correct. Possible solutions include: 20 quarters, 50 dimes, 10 quarters and 25 dimes.

2. 12:00; explanations will vary

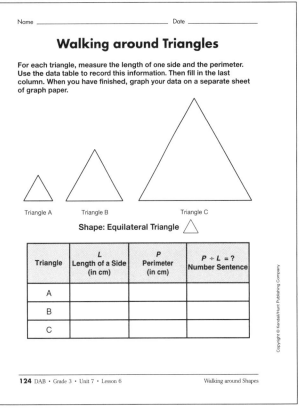

Name _____ Date _____

PART 3
Use base-ten shorthand or a shortcut method to solve the following problems. Estimate to make sure your answers are reasonable.

1. 3496
   + 707

2. 4357
   + 2828

3. 359
   − 176

4. 3001
   − 1998

5. Explain your estimation strategy for Question 4.
_____
_____
_____

PART 4
1. Shelby has $5.00 in her piggy bank. Her piggy bank only has coins inside. What coins might Shelby have that add up to $5.00? Give at least two examples.
_____

2. Jeffrey wants to visit his grandmother after his Little League game on Saturday. If his Little League game ends at 11:35 and it takes 25 minutes to travel to his grandmother's house, what time will Jeffrey begin his visit? _____ Show how you solved the problem.

EXPLORING MULTIPLICATION AND DIVISION   DAB • Grade 3 • Unit 7 **113**

Discovery Assignment Book - page 113

Discovery Assignment Book (p. 124)

Walking around Triangles

Figures 10 and 11 in the Lesson Guide show a completed data table and graph.†

Name _____ Date _____

Walking around Triangles

For each triangle, measure the length of one side and the perimeter. Use the data table to record this information. Then fill in the last column. When you have finished, graph your data on a separate sheet of graph paper.

Triangle A   Triangle B   Triangle C

Shape: Equilateral Triangle

Triangle	L Length of a Side (in cm)	P Perimeter (in cm)	P ÷ L = ? Number Sentence
A			
B			
C			

124 DAB • Grade 3 • Unit 7 • Lesson 6   Walking around Shapes

Discovery Assignment Book - page 124

*Answers for all the Home Practice in the *Discovery Assignment Book* are at the end of the unit.
†Answers and/or discussion are included in the Lesson Guide.

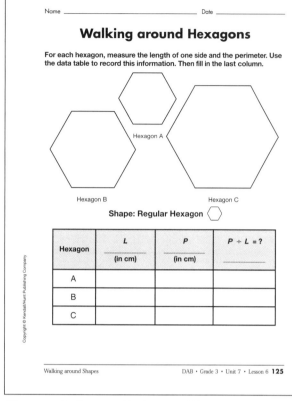

Discovery Assignment Book - page 125

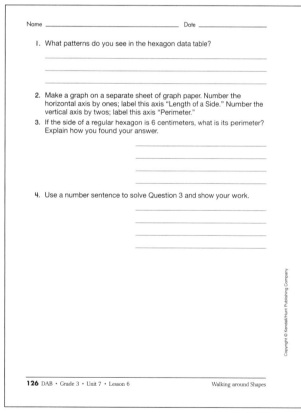

Discovery Assignment Book - page 126

Discovery Assignment Book (p. 125)

Walking around Hexagons

Hexagons	L Length of a Side (in cm)	P Perimeter (in cm)	P ÷ L = ? Number Sentence
A	2	12	12 ÷ 2 = 6
B	3	18	18 ÷ 3 = 6
C	4	24	24 ÷ 4 = 6

1. Possible patterns: The last column is always a 6. The perimeter is always 6 times a side.

Discovery Assignment Book (p. 126)

2.

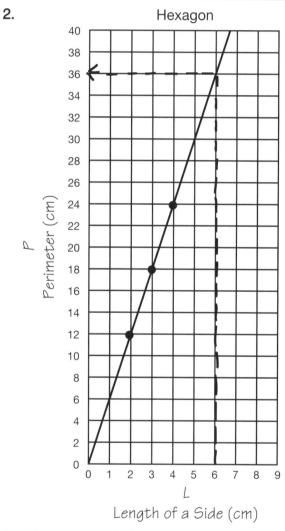

3. 36 cm; see graph for extrapolation*

4. 6 × 6 cm = 36 cm

*Answers and/or discussion are included in the Lesson Guide.

Discovery Assignment Book (p. 127)

Walking around Squares

Square	L Length of a Side (in cm)	P Perimeter (in cm)	P ÷ L = ? Number Sentence
A	1	4	$4 \div 1 = 4$
B	3	12	$12 \div 3 = 4$
C	9	36	$36 \div 9 = 4$

Discovery Assignment Book (p. 128)

1. Possible patterns: The last column is always a 4. The perimeter is always 4 times a side.

2.
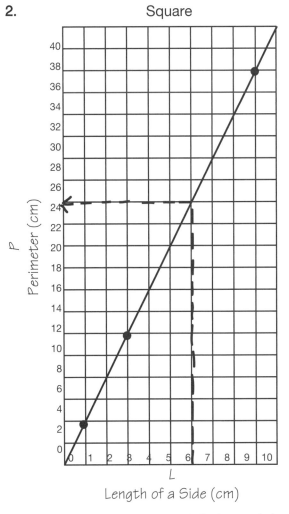

Square

3. 4×6 cm $= 24$ cm; see graph for interpolation

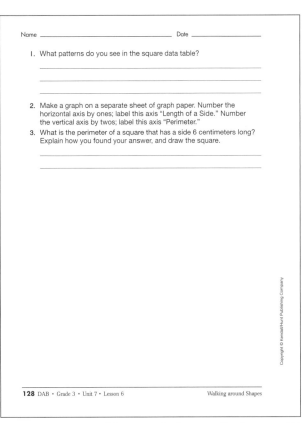

Discovery Assignment Book - page 127

Discovery Assignment Book - page 128

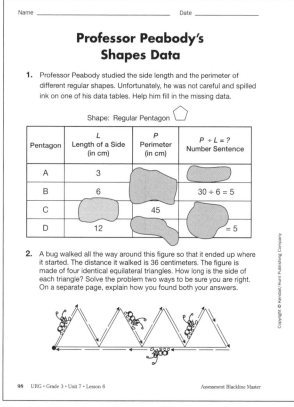

Unit Resource Guide (p. 98)

Professor Peabody's Shapes Data

1.

Pentagon	L Length of a Side (in cm)	P Perimeter (in cm)	P ÷ L = ? Number Sentence
A	3	15	15 ÷ 3 = 5
B	6	30	30 ÷ 6 = 5
C	9	45	45 ÷ 9 = 5
D	12	60	60 ÷ 12 = 5

2. 3 cm. Three possible ways: 36 cm ÷ 12 = 3 cm or 36 cm ÷ 4 = 9 cm; 9 cm is the perimeter of one triangle; 9 cm ÷ 3 = 3 cm; measure the figure with a ruler.

Unit Resource Guide - page 98

Discovery Assignment Book (p. 112)

Home Practice

Part 1

1. **A.** 25   **B.** 25   **C.** 25
2. **A.** 10   **B.** 20   **C.** 60
3. $(12 + 8) + 5 = 25$; $(17 + 3) + 5 = 25$; $5 + (16 + 4) = 25$; explanations will vary.

Part 2

1. **A.** 70   **B.** 60   **C.** 90
2. **A.** 200   **B.** 220   **C.** 240
3. **A.** $0.10   **B.** $0.05
4. 7 pencils; $50¢ \div 7¢ = 7$ with a remainder of $1¢$; strategies will vary.

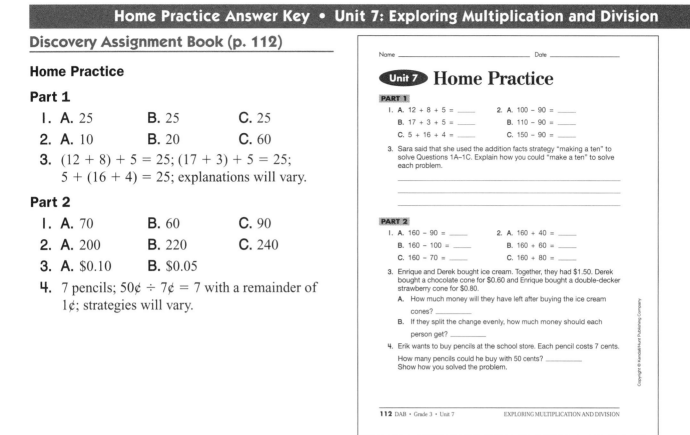

Discovery Assignment Book - page 112

Discovery Assignment Book (p. 113)

Part 3

1. 4203
2. 7185
3. 183
4. 1003
5. Strategies will vary. Possible strategy: $3000 - 2000 = 1000$

Part 4

1. Answers will vary. Any combination of coins that equal $5.00 is correct. Possible solutions include: 20 quarters, 50 dimes, 10 quarters and 25 dimes.
2. 12:00; explanations will vary.

Discovery Assignment Book - page 113

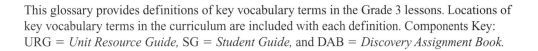

Glossary

This glossary provides definitions of key vocabulary terms in the Grade 3 lessons. Locations of key vocabulary terms in the curriculum are included with each definition. Components Key: URG = *Unit Resource Guide*, SG = *Student Guide*, and DAB = *Discovery Assignment Book.*

A

Area (URG Unit 5; SG Unit 5)
The area of a shape is the amount of space it covers, measured in square units.

Array (URG Unit 7 & Unit 11)
An array is an arrangement of elements into a rectangular pattern of (horizontal) rows and (vertical) columns. (*See* column and row.)

Associative Property of Addition (URG Unit 2)
For any three numbers a, b, and c we have $a + (b + c) = (a + b) + c$. For example in finding the sum of 4, 8, and 2, one can compute $4 + 8$ first and then add 2: $(4 + 8) + 2 = 14$. Alternatively, we can compute $8 + 2$ and then add the result to 4: $4 + (8 + 2) = 4 + 10 = 14$.

Average (URG Unit 5)
A number that can be used to represent a typical value in a set of data. (*See also* mean and median.)

Axes (URG Unit 8; SG Unit 8)
Reference lines on a graph. In the Cartesian coordinate system, the axes are two perpendicular lines that meet at the origin. The singular of axes is axis.

B

Base (of a cube model) (URG Unit 18; SG Unit 18)
The part of a cube model that sits on the "ground."

Base-Ten Board (URG Unit 4)
A tool to help children organize base-ten pieces when they are representing numbers.

Base-Ten Pieces (URG Unit 4; SG Unit 4)
A set of manipulatives used to model our number system as shown in the figure at the right. Note that a skinny is made of 10 bits, a flat is made of 100 bits, and a pack is made of 1000 bits.

Base-Ten Shorthand (SG Unit 4)
A pictorial representation of the base-ten pieces as shown.

Nickname	Picture	Shorthand
bit	⬚	.
skinny	▭	/
flat	▱	▱
pack	▧	▱

Best-Fit Line (URG Unit 9; SG Unit 9; DAB Unit 9)
The line that comes closest to the most number of points on a point graph.

Bit (URG Unit 4; SG Unit 4)
A cube that measures 1 cm on each edge. It is the smallest of the base-ten pieces that is often used to represent 1. (*See also* base-ten pieces.)

C

Capacity (URG Unit 16)
1. The volume of the inside of a container.
2. The largest volume a container can hold.

Cartesian Coordinate System (URG Unit 8)
A method of locating points on a flat surface by means of numbers. This method is named after its originator, René Descartes. (*See also* coordinates.)

Centimeter (cm)
A unit of measure in the metric system equal to one-hundredth of a meter. (1 inch = 2.54 cm)

Column (URG Unit 11)
In an array, the objects lined up vertically.

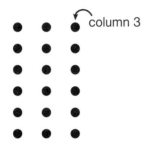

Common Fraction (URG Unit 15)
Any fraction that is written with a numerator and denominator that are whole numbers. For example, $\frac{3}{4}$ and $\frac{9}{4}$ are both common fractions. (*See also* decimal fraction.)

Commutative Property of Addition (URG Unit 2 & Unit 11)
This is also known as the Order Property of Addition. Changing the order of the addends does not change the sum. For example, $3 + 5 = 5 + 3 = 8$. Using variables, $n + m = m + n$.

Commutative Property of Multiplication (URG Unit 11)
Changing the order of the factors in a multiplication problem does not change the result, e.g., $7 \times 3 = 3 \times 7 = 21$. (*See also* turn-around facts.)

Congruent (URG Unit 12 & Unit 17; SG Unit 12)
Figures with the same shape and size.

Convenient Number (URG Unit 6)
A number used in computation that is close enough to give a good estimate, but is also easy to compute mentally, e.g., 25 and 30 are convenient numbers for 27.

Coordinates (URG Unit 8; SG Unit 8)
An ordered pair of numbers that locates points on a flat surface by giving distances from a pair of coordinate axes. For example, if a point has coordinates (4, 5) it is 4 units from the vertical axis and 5 units from the horizontal axis.

Counting Back (URG Unit 2)
A strategy for subtracting in which students start from a larger number and then count down until the number is reached. For example, to solve $8 - 3$, begin with 8 and count down three, 7, 6, 5.

Counting Down (*See* counting back.)

Counting Up (URG Unit 2)
A strategy for subtraction in which the student starts at the lower number and counts on to the higher number. For example, to solve $8 - 5$, the student starts at 5 and counts up three numbers (6, 7, 8). So $8 - 5 = 3$.

Cube (SG Unit 18)
A three-dimensional shape with six congruent square faces.

Cubic Centimeter (cc)
  (URG Unit 16; SG Unit 16)
The volume of a cube that is one centimeter long on each edge.

cubic centimeter

Cup (URG Unit 16)
A unit of volume equal to 8 fluid ounces, one-half pint.

D

Decimal Fraction (URG Unit 15)
A fraction written as a decimal. For example, 0.75 and 0.4 are decimal fractions and $\frac{75}{100}$ and $\frac{4}{10}$ are called common fractions. (*See also* fraction.)

Denominator (URG Unit 13)
The number below the line in a fraction. The denominator indicates the number of equal parts in which the unit whole is divided. For example, the 5 is the denominator in the fraction $\frac{2}{5}$. In this case the unit whole is divided into five equal parts.

Density (URG Unit 16)
The ratio of an object's mass to its volume.

Difference (URG Unit 2)
The answer to a subtraction problem.

Dissection (URG Unit 12 & Unit 17)
Cutting or decomposing a geometric shape into smaller shapes that cover it exactly.

Distributive Property of Multiplication over Addition
  (URG Unit 19)
For any three numbers *a, b,* and *c, a* $\times$ (*b* + *c*) = *a* $\times$ *b* + *a* $\times$ *c*. The distributive property is the foundation for most methods of multidigit multiplication. For example, $9 \times (17) = 9 \times (10 + 7) = 9 \times 10 + 9 \times 7 = 90 + 63 = 153$.

E

Equal-Arm Balance
See two-pan balance.

Equilateral Triangle (URG Unit 7)
A triangle with all sides of equal length and all angles of equal measure.

Equivalent Fractions (SG Unit 17)
Fractions that have the same value, e.g., $\frac{2}{4} = \frac{1}{2}$.

Estimate (URG Unit 5 & Unit 6)
1. (verb) To find *about* how many.
2. (noun) An approximate number.

Extrapolation (URG Unit 7)
Using patterns in data to make predictions or to estimate values that lie beyond the range of values in the set of data.

F

Fact Family (URG Unit 11; SG Unit 11)
Related math facts, e.g., $3 \times 4 = 12$, $4 \times 3 = 12$, $12 \div 3 = 4$, $12 \div 4 = 3$.

Factor (URG Unit 11; SG Unit 11)
1. In a multiplication problem, the numbers that are multiplied together. In the problem $3 \times 4 = 12$, 3 and 4 are the factors.
2. Whole numbers that can be multiplied together to get a number. That is, numbers that divide a number evenly, e.g., 1, 2, 3, 4, 6, and 12 are all the factors of 12.

Fewest Pieces Rule (URG Unit 4 & Unit 6; SG Unit 4)
Using the least number of base-ten pieces to represent a number. (*See also* base-ten pieces.)

Flat (URG Unit 4; SG Unit 4)
A block that measures 1 cm × 10 cm × 10 cm. It is one of the base-ten pieces that is often used to represent 100. (*See also* base-ten pieces.)

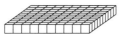

Flip (URG Unit 12)
A motion of the plane in which a figure is reflected over a line so that any point and its image are the same distance from the line.

Fraction (URG Unit 15)
A number that can be written as $\frac{a}{b}$ where a and b are whole numbers and b is not zero. For example, $\frac{1}{2}$, 0.5, and 2 are all fractions since 0.5 can be written as $\frac{5}{10}$ and 2 can be written as $\frac{2}{1}$.

Front-End Estimation (URG Unit 6)
Estimation by looking at the left-most digit.

G

Gallon (gal) (URG Unit 16)
A unit of volume equal to four quarts.

Gram
The basic unit used to measure mass.

H

Hexagon (SG Unit 12)
A six-sided polygon.

Horizontal Axis (SG Unit 1)
In a coordinate grid, the *x*-axis. The axis that extends from left to right.

I

Interpolation (URG Unit 7)
Making predictions or estimating values that lie between data points in a set of data.

J

K

Kilogram
1000 grams.

L

Likely Event (SG Unit 1)
An event that has a high probability of occurring.

Line of Symmetry (URG Unit 12)
A line is a line of symmetry for a plane figure if, when the figure is folded along this line, the two parts match exactly.

Line Symmetry (URG Unit 12; SG Unit 12)
A figure has line symmetry if it has at least one line of symmetry.

Liter (l) (URG Unit 16; SG Unit 16)
Metric unit used to measure volume. A liter is a little more than a quart.

M

Magic Square (URG Unit 2)
A square array of digits in which the sums of the rows, columns, and main diagonals are the same.

Making a Ten (URG Unit 2)
Strategies for addition and subtraction that make use of knowing the sums to ten. For example, knowing $6 + 4 = 10$ can be helpful in finding $10 - 6 = 4$ and $11 - 6 = 5$.

Mass (URG Unit 9 & Unit 16; SG Unit 9)
The amount of matter in an object.

Mean (URG Unit 5)
An average of a set of numbers that is found by adding the values of the data and dividing by the number of values.

Measurement Division (URG Unit 7)
Division as equal grouping. The total number of objects and the number of objects in each group are known. The number of groups is the unknown. For example, tulip bulbs come in packages of 8. If 216 bulbs are sold, how many packages are sold?

Measurement Error (URG Unit 9)
The unavoidable error that occurs due to the limitations inherent to any measurement instrument.

Median (URG Unit 5; DAB Unit 5)
For a set with an odd number of data arranged in order, it is the middle number. For an even number of data arranged in order, it is the number halfway between the two middle numbers.

Meniscus (URG Unit 16; SG Unit 16)
The curved surface formed when a liquid creeps up the side of a container (for example, a graduated cylinder).

Meter (m)
The standard unit of length measure in the metric system. One meter is approximately 39 inches.

Milliliter (ml) (URG Unit 16; SG Unit 16)
A measure of capacity in the metric system that is the volume of a cube that is one centimeter long on each edge.

Multiple (URG Unit 3 & Unit 11)
A number is a multiple of another number if it is evenly divisible by that number. For example, 12 is a multiple of 2 since 2 divides 12 evenly.

N

Numerator (URG Unit 13)
The number written above the line in a fraction. For example, the 2 is the numerator in the fraction $\frac{2}{5}$. (*See also* denominator.)

O

One-Dimensional Object (URG Unit 18; SG Unit 18)
An object is one-dimensional if it is made up of pieces of lines and curves.

Ordered Pairs (URG Unit 8)
A pair of numbers that gives the coordinates of a point on a grid in relation to the origin. The horizontal coordinate is given first; the vertical coordinate is given second. For example, the ordered pair (5, 3) tells us to move five units to the right of the origin and 3 units up.

Origin (URG Unit 8)
The point at which the *x*- and *y*-axes (horizontal and vertical axes) intersect on a coordinate plane. The origin is described by the ordered pair (0, 0) and serves as a reference point so that all the points on the plane can be located by ordered pairs.

P

Pack (URG Unit 4; SG Unit 4)
A cube that measures 10 cm on each edge. It is one of the base-ten pieces that is often used to represent 1000. (*See also* base-ten pieces.)

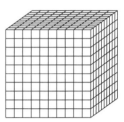

Palindrome (URG Unit 6)
A number, word, or phrase that reads the same forward and backward, e.g., 12321.

Parallel Lines (URG Unit 18)
Lines that are in the same direction. In the plane, parallel lines are lines that do not intersect.

Parallelogram (URG Unit 18)
A quadrilateral with two pairs of parallel sides.

Partitive Division (URG Unit 7)
Division as equal sharing. The total number of objects and the number of groups are known. The number of objects in each group is the unknown. For example, Frank has 144 marbles that he divides equally into 6 groups. How many marbles are in each group?

Pentagon (SG Unit 12)
A five-sided, five-angled polygon.

Perimeter (URG Unit 7; DAB Unit 7)
The distance around a two-dimensional shape.

Pint (URG Unit 16)
A unit of volume measure equal to 16 fluid ounces, i.e., two cups.

Polygon
A two-dimensional connected figure made of line segments in which each endpoint of every side meets with an endpoint of exactly one other side.

Population (URG Unit 1; SG Unit 1)
A collection of persons or things whose properties will be analyzed in a survey or experiment.

Prediction (SG Unit 1)
Using data to declare or foretell what is likely to occur.

Prime Number (URG Unit 11)
A number that has exactly two factors. For example, 7 has exactly two distinct factors, 1 and 7.

Prism
A three-dimensional figure that has two congruent faces, called bases, that are parallel to each other, and all other faces are parallelograms.

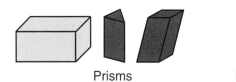

Prisms   Not a prism

Product (URG Unit 11; SG Unit 11; DAB Unit 11)
The answer to a multiplication problem. In the problem $3 \times 4 = 12$, 12 is the product.

Q

Quadrilateral (URG Unit 18)
A polygon with four sides.

Quart (URG Unit 16)
A unit of volume equal to 32 fluid ounces; one quarter of a gallon.

R

Recording Sheet (URG Unit 4)
A place value chart used for addition and subtraction problems.

Rectangular Prism (URG Unit 18; SG Unit 18)
A prism whose bases are rectangles. A right rectangular prism is a prism having all faces rectangles.

Regular (URG Unit 7; DAB Unit 7)
A polygon is regular if all sides are of equal length and all angles are equal.

Remainder (URG Unit 7)
Something that remains or is left after a division problem. The portion of the dividend that is not evenly divisible by the divisor, e.g., $16 \div 5 = 3$ with 1 as a remainder.

Right Angle (SG Unit 12)
An angle that measures 90°.

Rotation (turn) (URG Unit 12)
A transformation (motion) in which a figure is turned a specified angle and direction around a point.

Row (URG Unit 11)
In an array, the objects lined up horizontally.

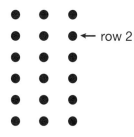

Rubric (URG Unit 2)
A written guideline for assigning scores to student work, for the purpose of assessment.

S

Sample (URG Unit 1; SG Unit 1)
A part or subset of a population.

Skinny (URG Unit 4; SG Unit 4)
A block that measures 1 cm $\times$ 1 cm $\times$ 10 cm. It is one of the base-ten pieces that is often used to represent 10. (*See also* base-ten pieces.)

Square Centimeter (sq cm) (SG Unit 5)
The area of a square that is 1 cm long on each side.

Square Number (SG Unit 11)
A number that is the product of a whole number multiplied by itself. For example, 25 is a square number since $5 \times 5 = 25$. A square number can be represented by a square array with the same number of rows as columns. A square array for 25 has 5 rows of 5 objects in each row or 25 total objects.

Standard Masses
A set of objects with convenient masses, usually 1 g, 10 g, 100 g, etc.

Sum (URG Unit 2; SG Unit 2)
The answer to an addition problem.

Survey (URG Unit 14; SG Unit 14)
An investigation conducted by collecting data from a sample of a population and then analyzing it. Usually surveys are used to make predictions about the entire population.

T

Tangrams (SG Unit 12)
A type of geometric puzzle. A shape is given and it must be covered exactly with seven standard shapes called tans.

Thinking Addition (URG Unit 2)
A strategy for subtraction that uses a related addition problem. For example, $15 - 7 = 8$ because $8 + 7 = 15$.

Three-Dimensional (URG Unit 18; SG Unit 18)
Existing in three-dimensional space; having length, width, and depth.

TIMS Laboratory Method (URG Unit 1; SG Unit 1)
A method that students use to organize experiments and investigations. It involves four components: draw, collect, graph, and explore. It is a way to help students learn about the scientific method.

Turn (URG Unit 12)
(*See* rotation.)

Turn-Around Facts (URG Unit 2 & Unit 11 p. 37; SG Unit 11)
Addition facts that have the same addends but in a different order, e.g., $3 + 4 = 7$ and $4 + 3 = 7$. (*See also* commutative property of addition and commutative property of multiplication.)

Two-Dimensional (URG Unit 18; SG Unit 18)
Existing in the plane; having length and width.

Two-Pan Balance
A device for measuring the mass of an object by balancing the object against a number of standard masses (usually multiples of 1 unit, 10 units, and 100 units, etc.).

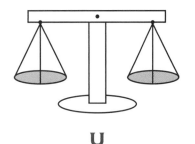

U

Unit (of measurement) (URG Unit 18)
A precisely fixed quantity used to measure. For example, centimeter, foot, kilogram, and quart are units of measurement.

Using a Ten (URG Unit 2)
1. A strategy for addition that uses partitions of the number 10. For example, one can find $8 + 6$ by thinking $8 + 6 = 8 + 2 + 4 = 10 + 4 = 14$.
2. A strategy for subtraction that uses facts that involve subtracting 10. For example, students can use $17 - 10 = 7$ to learn the "close fact" $17 - 9 = 8$.

Using Doubles (URG Unit 2)
Strategies for addition and subtraction that use knowing doubles. For example, one can find $7 + 8$ by thinking $7 + 8 = 7 + 7 + 1 = 14 + 1 = 15$. Knowing $7 + 7 = 14$ can be helpful in finding $14 - 7 = 7$ and $14 - 8 = 6$.

V

Value (URG Unit 1; SG Unit 1)
The possible outcomes of a variable. For example, red, green, and blue are possible values for the variable *color*. Two meters and 1.65 meters are possible values for the variable *length*.

Variable (URG Unit 1; SG Unit 1)
1. An attribute or quantity that changes or varies.
2. A symbol that can stand for a variable.

Vertex (URG Unit 12; SG Unit 12)
1. A point where the sides of a polygon meet.
2. A point where the edges of a three-dimensional object meet.

Vertical Axis (SG Unit 1)
In a coordinate grid, the y-axis. It is perpendicular to the horizontal axis.

Volume (URG Unit 16; SG Unit 16)
The measure of the amount of space occupied by an object.

Volume by Displacement (URG Unit 16)
A way of measuring volume of an object by measuring the amount of water (or some other fluid) it displaces.

W

Weight (URG Unit 9)
A measure of the pull of gravity on an object. One unit for measuring weight is the pound.

X

Y

Z